THE SIKH PSYCHE

A study of the fictional writings of
Bhai Vir Singh

Aḥaraṇ(i) mat(i) ved(u) hathīār(u)
—Jap(u)

THE SIKH PSYCHE

A STUDY OF THE FICTIONAL WRITINGS OF BHAI VIR SINGH

DR. HARCHARAN SINGH SOBTI
M.A. (Panjabi); M.A. (Philosophy);
LL. B; Ph.D. (Buddhist Studies)

Eastern Book Linkers
DELHI :: (INDIA)

Published by
EASTERN BOOK LINKERS
5825, New Chandrawal, Jawahar Nagar,
Delhi-110007

First Edition : 1990

Price EASTERN BOOK LINKERS EBL Rs. 300 -

ISBN—81-85133-42-5

Printed by :

Amar Printing Press (Sham Printing Agency),
8/25, Vijay Nagar, Double Storey, Delhi-110009

DEDICATED

to

His Holiness Baba Ajit Singh Ji Chaggar
with reverence and gratitude

PREFACE

Sometimes in the year 1982, I presented a paper on 'Bhai Vir Singh : A Study in Paradox' (later included in my book *Studies in Panjabi Fiction* (1987) and which forms the part of Chapter 6 of the present book) in the seminar on Bhai Vir Singh, attended by 'one kind' of audience. The paper was not only received without cheers, but with cold indifference that prompted me to develope the paper in the form of a book. But that was not the only reason. In fact, my experiences as a member of Panjabi academic community also inspired me while giving the present shape to the book.

There are quite a few Mir Mannu in Panjabi academic world One such Mir Mannu adopted, proportionately, quite a few, more or less, similar measures that Mir Mannu made use of against the Sikh community. During this 'Term of Trial', I felt, as if the rebellious spirit of the Sikh community pitted against Mir Mannu was taking a new shape, in microcosmic form, in my Being and this realization always kept me in high spirits (*caṛdi kalā*), rooted in the Sikh tradition.

I am not scared of being misunderstood, at times, I prefer that. But, it is good for you to keep in mind that the present book is based on Bhai Sahib's trilogy and my assessment of the author is confined to one phase, rather, the earliest phase of his writings.

Bhai Vir Singh, in the last decade of nineteenth century, viewed the turbulent period in the history of the Sikhs during first half of the eighteenth century, to boost the morale of the Sikhs and *also* to put them on the right hand side of the British Masters. I am writing this book in the last decade of twentieth century, and my job is more difficult. I had to assess the entire Sikh movement, right from its commencement, including the Singh Sabha movement, and I am living in the turbulent period of the Sikh history.

Notwithstanding our best intentions to guard against printing errors, number of errors have escaped our notice. We hope that these errors would be corrected with ease with the help of errata given at the end of the book.

Translations of Panjabi and Urdu quotations are by the author unless specified, otherwise.

6th, June 1990
D13A/30 Model Town, HARCHARAN SINGH SOBTI
Delhi-110009 (India).

ACKNOWLEDGEMENTS

For writing Chapter 3 I am, especially, indebted to Dr. Hari Ram Gupta, Sardar Khushwant Singh and Dr. Gopal Singh.

I am grateful to Dr. S. M. Abbas Sharib Rudaulvi Department of Urdu, University of Delhi, for the source of information regarding the payment received by Maulvi Muhammad Najmulghani, from the British Masters, commissioned to malign Nawab Vajid Ali Shah.

I consider it my pleasant duty to thank Shri Sher Singh, Deputy Librarian, University of Delhi for his valuable guidance in the matters of bibliography; and to Shri J. B. Khanna, the Assistant Librarian, for his timely and willing co-operation.

I am in no way less indcbted to Miss Navneet Lamba, Librarian, Bhai Vir Singh Sahitya Sadan, New Delhi, for making available, for consultation, some of the rare issues of *Khalsa Samacar*.

I feel highly obliged to Sardar Waryam Singh, Librarian, S. G. T. B. Khalsa College, University of Delhi, for very kindly allowing me to use the Library.

My special thanks due to Shri Deepak Malhotra, Principal, Dyal Singh (Evening) College, University of Delhi, for his gracious interest in my academic pursuits and in the publication of this book.

Not to express my gratitude towards Professor Fazl-ul-Haque, Department of Urdu, University of Delhi, with whom I occasionally discussed the design and the details of the book, is simply to keep it out of the framework of formalities.

I am also grateful to M/s. Eastern Book Linkers, New Delhi, for having very kindly published this book.

HSS

CONTENTS

CHAPTER I

THE SURVEY OF THE LITERATURE

The fictional writings of Bhai Vir Singh (1872-1957) *viz.* *Sundri* (1898),[1] *Bijay Singh* (1899-1900)[2] and *Satwant Kaur* (1900, 1927),[3] generally referred to as novels or historical romances, mainly, depict the ethos of the Sikh community of the Panjab, struggling for its survival and the retention of identity, during the later Mughal period of Indian history. These writings, therefore, are of the nature of collage and, simultaneously, fall in the purview of literature, religion and history. The evaluation of these writings commenced, nearly, four decades after the time of their publications, *i.e.* in early forties and in the pre-Partition days of India, later on, cut into Bharat and Pakistan, in the year 1947. Surinder Singh Kohli in his *Panjabi Sahit Da Itihas*, published in June, 1943, described, "the characterization of these three novels duly affected by the spirit of the times."[4] "Such novels were also in vogue in Urdu and Bengali languages," adds Kohli "in which one indulged in condemning other's religion by painting it ferocious, thus spreading ill-will against it."[5] Kohli viewed the spirit of these writings in a wider perspective and found that it was quite in conformity with the then prevailing 'climate of opinion.' This means that the virus of communalism had already polluted the life of Indian people that found its reflection in Indian novel and which in turn adversely affected the communal harmony.

Gopal Singh, like Kohli, in his *Panjabi Sahit Da Itihas* published in 1946 in Panjabi language and in Persian Script, also touched upon the art of characterization of these writings providing some more informations. Gopal Singh, while specifying the flaw in the art of characterization, has pointed out that "the characters depicted fall short of characteristics of the normal human beings, rather they represent beings classified into categories."[6] In support of his contention, he adds, that "all the Sikhs are depicted brave alike, infused with the spirit of service, helpful to one and all including their enemies; while all the Hindus are portrayed spineless as if serving time. And, the Muslims [*Sic*] are identified as if bent upon committing atrocities."[7] Bhai Sahib, opines Gopal Singh, "is not to be blamed for this kind of schematic characterization. An existing flaws owe much to the epoch he belonged to or it can be discredited to the motive that prompted these writings."[8] Again, "it was the period of communal frenzy and it was normal," submits Gopal Singh, "to do communal writings."[9] "Abdul Halim Sharar" informs Gopal Singh, "in those days was writing historical novels in Urdu, exclusively concerned with Muslim history."[10] In Bengali Bankim Chandra Chatterji wrote his famous novel *Anandamaṭh* which Gopal Singh has characterized as "an anti-Muslim writing."[11] In brief, Gopal Singh toes the line of Kohli and upholds, that the fictional writings of Bhai Vir Singh, constitute a mirror, reflecting the spirit of times, faithfully.

Kohli only hinted at the prevalent tone of novel-writing in some of the Indian languages, whereas, Gopal Singh elaborated it and, thus, made certain observations which call for detailed analysis prior to arriving at any conclusion. Here, we may add that later on Kohli while commenting on these writings, in his article, "Bhai Vir Singh's Novel" (1973), hardly holds views different from Gopal Singh, when the former states :

> The writer creates such situations, as to make a convincing beginning regarding the pious lives of the Sikhs and immoral and ferocious attitude of the Muslims. [*Sic*].[12]

In fact, it is Turk/Mughal the Ruler, who is depicted as a villain in these writings of Bhai Vir Singh and not the Muslim, as contended by Kohli and Gopal Singh. A clear-cut distinction to that effect is available, throughout the texts of these writings. We quote a few instances :

i. *Sundri* : Surasati (later on Sundri) has been abducted by a Mughal and she is in his captivity. Some of the family members of Surasati alongwith the *Paṅca* of the village approach the Mughal, bargain with him and appeal to him for the release of Surasati. The Mughal refuses to hand-over Surasati to them. Then, Surasati manages to convey to her brother that,

   Stand up ! go to your home, my Brother ! [Don't Worry] I shall not drink *Mughal's Water* [and prefer] to burn myself alive.[13]

ii. *Sundri* : After the abduction of Surasati by a Mughal, the kith and kin of Surasati assemble to console the family-members. It is in these set of circumstances that the author draws a distinction between Mughal and the Muslims, when he states : *Hindus and Muslims* both expressed their agony and condemned it as an act of stark injustice,[14]

iii. *Bijay Singh* : In *Bijay Singh*, Ram Lal has become Bijay Singh, the *Khālsā*. His mother is scared of the Turks who are cruel and unjust and is worried about the future of her son. Bijay Singh tries to console his mother but the latter is adamant and wants that Bijay Singh should do away with *Keś* (unshorn hair). To substantiate the validity of her fears, she quotes a reference from the Sikh history and asks :

> You tell me, in what way Bhai Mani Singh of Amritsar harmed the Turks ? Persons of such a equanimous vision are hard to find, *who would show equal regard to all the Hindus and Muslims* visiting him. But, then, the Turks [you know in what way] mercilessly butchered him. The same way, my son ! I am afraid you may not meet the same fate.[15]

iv. *Satwant Kaur* : In *Satwant Kaur* the author draws an unimbiguous distinction between Abdali the alien and the Muslims, who constitute an integral part of the native population. In the words of the author :

> They [the Sikhs] were filled with anger on this account that why they should interfere with other's affairs. Let Abdali live [peacefully] in his own country. What business has he to come to Hindustan, [with a view] to plunder and destroy it ? *But, they did not find Hindus and Muslims around them united to fight against common enemy.* Therefore, they had to bear the sufferings, all alone. We must lead our country to freedom. We want to see our country prosperous and for that we must have our own *Rāj* (rule). This idea, like a liquor, had gone to the heads of the Sikhs.[16]

So, the contempt depicted in the fictional writings of Bhai Vir Singh, is for the inside Ruler or for the outside plunderer or aggressor. The Muslims are not less than brethren Kohli and Gopal Singh, both, misread Turk/Mughal as Muslims and failed to distinguish between Ruling elite and the people.

Gopal Singh's reference to Abdul Halim Sharar needs a little elaboration. Abdul Halim Sharar (1860-1926) is considered 'the pioneer of the historical romances in Urdu' and is eulogized as 'Sir Walter Scott of Urdu Novel.' Sharar wrote a good number of novels. Some of his novels *e. g. Mulikul-Aziz Verjina, Mansur-Mohna, Firdos-e-Baren, Aiyyam-e-Arab* and *Badrunnisa ki musibat etc.* are thematically quite significant. Sharar, according to Aijaz Hussain, in his novels described the heydays of Islam, victories of his ancestors and defeats of other nationalities which proved highly satisfying for the Muslims who had lost their kingdom of Hindustan. Also, these novels injected the spirit of self-esteem among the Muslims.[17] R. Russell has pointed out to yet another aspect of Sharar's novels. "Stated in the broadest terms," writes Russel in his article, "The Development of the Modern Novel in Urdu" (1970), "they all have a single theme—the portrayal of the glorious past of Islam and of the great superiority of Islamic civilization in its heyday over that of contemporary non-Muslims (especially) Christian powers."[18] To undermine rather to malign Christians, "Sexual lust, allied with religious fanaticism, is portrayed as the dominant motive of the Christian characters."[19] In what way the above two characteristic features of Sharar's novels had an impact on Muslim readers is beautifully summed up by Faiz Ahmad Faiz (1911-1984) which reads as :

> ... the recital of past conquest partly inspired them

> [Muslims] with self-respect and partly with emotienal solace, with the thought that even if they were not heroes at least their forefathers had been...the description of the vices of other peoples provided them with a way of taking mental revenge for their present subjection......[20]

Sharar's novels armed the Muslim readers with the moral strength to resist the temptation of following the life-style of the Ruler, the Britisher in the present case.

As regard to *Anandamaṭh*, first time searlized in the journal *Baṅgadarshan* during 1880-82 and 'after substantial changes', published in the form of a book, in the year 1882, T. W. Clark while writing on "Bengali Prose Fiction up to Bankimcandra" (1970), categorically states that,

> .. ...In the later novels, Bankim's attitude towards Muslims [*Sic*] is hostile. In *Anandamaṭh* and *Sitaram* (1887) particularly they are *par-excellence* the enemy. They are portrayed as cowardly and cruel, rapicious and tyrannical. The heroes were Hindus, the villains Muslims......[21]

Later on, Sharif Ahmad,[22] while commenting upon Bankim in his doctoral thesis, verbatim reproduced the above cited quotation in affirmation.

Let us look into historical background and the relevant portion of the text of *Anandamaṭh*, to ascertain the truth about Bankim's (1838-1894) 'hostility towards Muslims.' The novel is set in the background of terrible famine that outbroke in Bengal in the Bengali year 1175 corresponding to 177(A.C. which carried away more than a third of its population. This calamity occurred during John Carter's government, about two years prior to the oppointment of Warren Hastings as a

Governor of Bengal in the year 1772. The province of Bengal, at that time, was not under British rule. In fact, there existed some kind of diarchy. The English, then, only collected the taxes and were absolutely under no obligation to protect the life and property of the people of Bengal. This responsibility laid upon Mir Jaffar (d. 1765) the *Nawāb* of Bengal, who in the words of Bankim was, "despicable traitor and disgrace to humanity......incapable of protecting even himself......took opium and slept......as for the people of Bengal they wept and went to destruction."[23] *Nawāb* is here condemned because he falls short of the expectations of his *ryot* or Subject. At one place, Bhavanda tells Mohendra Singh that,

> In every country the relation with the ruler is that of protector and protected; but what protection do our Mussalman rulers give us ? Our religion is destroyed, our caste defiled, our honour polluted, our family honour shamed; and now our very lives are going the same way. Unless we drive out these vice-besodden longbeards, the Hinduism of Hindus is doomed.[24]

Note the expression 'our Mussalman rulers.' The Ruler is villain; and it has nothing to do with the Mussalman as a community. As already stated that *Baṅgadarshan* version of *Anandamaṭh* was published 'only after substantial changes' in the form of a book in 1882. Referring to these 'substantial changes' Sisir Kumar Das points out that,

> In the first edition Bhabananda complains, our *rājā* (king) does not protect the people' (1. x). But in the fourth edition the word '*rājā*' is substituted by the word 'Musalman', obviously to tone down the criticism of the British administration.[25]

Similarly,

> The first version mentions the defeat of a group of English soliders by the *Santāns* but in the subsequent versions the word English is replaced by '*Sepoy*.'[26]

Again,

> The *Baṅgadarshan* version as well as the first edition of the novel refers to Jibananda's opponents as 'English'. But in the next edition 'English' was replaced by '*Yaban*' and in some places by '*nede*' both terms implying the Muslims, the second term being a pejorative one.[27]

Also,

> The word '*ingreder*' (of the English), which occurs in Chapter VIII, part iii in the first edition, was changed to '*Shatruder*' (of the enemies).

The 'substantial changes', thus, made are vocal enough. But, Sisir Kumar Das guarding against the temptation of deriving hasty conclusions warns, that,

> It must not be thought, however, that Bankim replaced all references to 'English' by 'Muslim.' Many references, positively anti-British and in consonance with the patriotic fervour of the *Santāns*, still remained unchanged in the book and they made it politically dangerous.[29]

The substantial changes made in the subsequent editions of *Anandamaṭh* hardly prove that Bankim was hostile towards the Muslims as an ethnic group. Rather, he was against the Muslim Rulcrs, in one form or the other. And, it is also true, that Bankim, in a way, was anti-British Rule, although, in the opinion of Sisir Kumar Das, "he was not courageous enough to ventilate his anti-British feelings openly."[30]

So, Gopal Singh and T. W. Clark, both, while concluding *Anandamaṭh* as anti-Muslim, made an error of judgement due to faulty perception coloured with biased considerations for different reasons. The theory of motive as advocated by Gopal Singh in defence of Bhai Vir Singh holds true to the extent that motive is invariably rooted in the soil of milieu. But, what matters is the author's analysis of the social forces operating in a given milieu and his *loyalities.*

Sharif Ahmad's acceptance of Clark's views on *Anandmaṭh* as an anti-Muslim writing, without examining it, is an examplary case of both the laxity in the field of scholarship and willingly falling a prey to communal frenzy.

Sant Singh Sekhon in his book *Bhai Vir Singh Te una Da Yug* (1962), at one place, repeates the same mistake committed by Kohli and Gopal Singh, when he writes that,

> He [Bhai Vir Singh] has always and at all times depicted the Sikh characters as idealists and Hindu and Muslim [*Sic*] characters in ugly form.

Sekhon, although a known Marxist literary critic, like Kohli and Gopal Singh, failed to look into the class-contents of these characters and consequent upon that the distinction (which is already there in the fictional writings) between the Ruler and the people (or ruled) got blurred. It is hardly an occasion for surprise. Indian Marxists, by and large, not yet de-classed, we find deep down in their hearts and minds, wedded to the inherited communal and other similar sentiments, which find outlet and reveal their true nature in the moments of 'relaxation.' At another place, in the same book, Sekhon adhering to Marxian approach to the study of literature, expressed his views about the overall merit/demerit of the fictional writings (he prefers to call historical romances) stating that,

> ......The causes of Mughal-Sikh conflict, as Bhai Vir Singh understands neither pertain to the economic of life nor they are of political nature; the basic reason is the atrocities committed by the Mughal ruling class and the religious protest of the Sikhs against these atrocities.[32]

Thus, according to Sekhon, the Sikhs as depicted in these writings were fighting a religious battle against only the atrocities of the Mughal Rulers, altogether devoid of any economic and political contents.

Surinder Singh Dusanjh in one of the chapters of his book *Panjabi Itihask Novel* (1969), while analysing the class-contents of these writings, pointed out that,

> In this way, the war between the Sikhs and the Muslims [*Sic*], in fact, was the war of peasantry and labour-class against the atrocities of the ruling class. Now, (18th century) for the first time, the Panjabi peasant, in the form of the Sikhs, started organised struggle against the ruling class, which acquired inviogration as a result of increasing atrocities of the Mughals.[33]

The Sikh-movement, therefore, was the movement of peasantry and labour class against the Mughals, the Rulers of the country. It is hard to concede that such a movement, as Sekhon contends, could have been devoid of economic and political contents.

As regard to the class-character of these writings Amarjot Sekhon puts forth, yet a new and *enlightening* observations. "Bhai Vir Singh", writes Amarjot in her book, *Panjabi Novel Da Itihas* (1972), "has taken up Sikh history as a subject matter in these novels, but has served the interests of middle class."[34] Elaborating her point she states that "all the characters of his novels come from the middle class. And, Bhai Vir Singh has depicted the life of middle class shop-keepers as a prototypal of the Sikh-movement."[35]

Here, the problem to identify the class-character of the Sikh movement as depicted in these writings, crops up, that needs dispassionate scrutiny, we propose to do in the following pages.

Some critics have also referred to the possibility of influence of Sir Walter Scott (1771-1832) on Bhai Vir Singh in matters of following the model of novel-writing. Only, Sekhon has come forward with crisp formulation that opens a new horizon of evaluating the significance of fictional writings of Bhai Vir Singh in historial perspective. Sekhon is of the view that,

> Bhai Vir Singh clearly follows the tradition of the historical novel perfected by Sir Walter Scott. And the fact of Sir Walter Scott undertaking to celebrate the heroism of a politically defeated nationality, the Scotts, must surely have appealed to Bhai Vir Singh as model to follow. In those last years of the nineteenth century the Sikhs of the Panjab, inspite of their defeat at the hands of the British were indeed lionised by their conquerors. And, it would not be far-fetched to say that they could share in the glory and greatness of the British empire very much as the Scotts were doing.[36]

Sekhon has bracketed the Sikhs of the last years of the nineteenth century with the Scotts. Both the nationalities had suffered defeat at the hands of Britishers.

What emerges from the above survey is that Bhai Vir Singh's fictional writings are not anti-Muslims directed against

Muslims as an ethnic group but these are definitely anti-Muslim Rulers—Rulers of the Past. Now, the Britishers had firmly established their rule in India. What was Bhai Sahib's attitude towards the Britishers – the Rulers of the Present ? This is the querry we are deeply concerned with.

References and Notes

1. (i) Harbans Singh, while referring to the time of writing and publication of *Sundri*, in his book, *Bhai Vir Singh* on page 38, states :

   > Bhai Vir Singh had conceived the story and written at least a portion of it while still at school. But it was not published untill 1898...

   (ii) According to Bhai Jodh Singh *Sundri* was written in 1896. Master Tara Singh, the leader of the Sikhs, according to Bhai Jodh Singh became Sikh after reading *Sundri*.

   See : Bhai Jodh Singh, "Bhai Vir Singh Te Singh Sabha Lehar" in S. S. Kohli (Ed.) *Bhai Vir Singh, Jiwan, Sama Te Racna*, p. 48.

   (iii) See : Appendix I to *Sundri*, 32nd Edition : September, 1966 p. 130.

2. *Bijay Singh* was published in two parts. The first part was published in 1899 and the second part in 1900.

3. Like *Bijay Singh, Satwant Kaur* was also published in two parts : Part one in 1900 and Part two in 1927.

   First part of *Satwant Kaur* was also serialized in *Khalsa Smacar*, in 1900 and the second part in the year 1927.

4-5. Surinder Singh Kohli, *Panjabi Sahit Da Itihas* p. 625.

6-11. Gopal Singh, *Panjabi Sahit Da Itihas* p. 352.

12. Gurbachan Singh Talib (Ed.) *Bhai Vir Singh Life Time and Work* p. 150.

13. *Sundri* 32nd Edition p. 6
14. *Idem.*
15. *Bijay Singh* 22nd Edition : September, 1967. p. 9.
16. *Satwant Kaur* Edition : March 1968. p. 311.
17. Aijaz Hussain, *Adabi Rujhanat* 5th Edition : May 1957, p. 234.
18. T. W. Clark (Ed.) *The Novel in India*, p. 123.
19. *Ibid.* p. 129.
20. Faiz Ahmad Faiz *Mizan, Nashirin* Lahore, 1962, Quoted in T. W. Clark (Ed.) *op. cit* p. 132.
21. T. W. Clark (Ed.) *op. cit.* p. 64.
22. Sharif Ahmad, *Abdul Halim Sharar : Life and His Works* p. 180.
23. Sri Aurbindo (Tr.) *Sri Aurbindo Birth Centenary Volume* 8, p. 331.
24. *Ibid* p. 340.
25. Sisir Kumar Das, *The Artist in Chains : The Life of Bankim Chandra Chatterji*, p. 141.

26-29. *Ibid.* p. 142

30. *Ibid.* p. 147
31. Sant Singh Sekhon, *Bhai Vir Singh Te Una Da Yug* p. 57.
32. *Ibid.* p. 73
33. Surinder Singh Dusanjh, *Panjabi Itihasak Novel*, p. 42.

34-35. Amarjot Sekhon, *Panjabi Novel Da Itihas* p. 37

36. Sant Singh Sekhon, "Bhai Vir Singh—The Father of Modern Panjabi Prose" in Gurbachan Singh Talib (Ed.) *op. cit.* p. 120.

CHAPTER 2

SIKHISM : THE RELIGION OF THE REBELS

The Sikhs, in the fictional writings of Bhai Vir Singh, are depicted as Rebels against the State. At times, opinions are borrowed and propagated without examining them. This kind of laxity, sometimes, lends an unwarranted support to the mischiefs or genuine but unsound judgements. To understand the exact nature of the rebellious spirit of the Sikhs, it is imperative, therefore, to look into the canonical and non-canonical Sikh literature and Sikh tradition, besides examining the opinions of the scholars on the subject.

Guru Nanak (1469-1539) the Founder-Guru of the Sikh tradition, like Buddha, (6th B.C.) did not deliver discourses, but sang in the praise of God and occasionally expressed his critical views on contemporary style of Indian life. Thus, prompted by the necessity of expressions gave shape to his transcendental experience making use of available material from the prevailing religious culture. An experience may be transcendental but its expression (in case it is not through Silence) is bound to be temporal. Two religious cultures *viz* Hindu and Islamic dominated the life of Indian people. The scholars interested in the Sikh tradition have conceived its origin in the background of these religious cultures and as expected have viewed it differently. "It is a mistake" writes Ernest Trumpp (1828-1885) in his prefactary remarks to the translation of *The Ādi Granth* (1877) "if Nanak is represented as having endeavoured to unite the Hindu and

Muhammadan idea about God."[1] "Nanak" in the words of Trumpp" remained a thorough Hindu.[2]" Gokul Chand Narang (d. 1969) characterizes Sikhism as an "embodiment of Hindu reaction against Islam."[3] Gurbachan Singh Talib subscribes to the similar views only his perception is of different kind. His observation is mainly focussed on the general phenomenon of 'accepting the new teaching of the Gurus. "In its ethnic origin" states Talib in the appendix entitled "Sikh-Hindu Relations Through History" to his book, *Guru Nanak : His Personality and Vision* ((1969), "Sikhism of course grew within Hinduism. Almost all who followed the Sikh teaching in the earlier days were Hindus. While accepting the new teaching of the Gurus, they might perhaps not even be conscious that they were changing one 'faith' for another. No such radical transition was involved in the process."[4] An acceptance of teaching of the Guru means the transformation of one's Being. Talib, it appears, has observed the phenomenon at a superficial level.

W. H. Mcleod finds the origin of Sikh tradition in Sant tradition and advocates the views of other independent iufluences as relatively slight.[5] Stephen Dunning in his paper, "The Sikh Religion : An Examination of Some of the Western Studies" (1970) while commenting upon Mcleod's thesis of the case against Muslim influences, writes that :

> The significanse of Mcleod's minimization of Muslim influence upon Guru Nanak pertains not so much to each specific concept or image which he discusses as to the general implication that Sikhism is really only a sectarian reform movement within Hinduism.[6]

A number of historians of medieval Indian Culture subscribe to the views that Sikhism is nothing but a synthesis between Hinduism and Islam.

Jawaharlal Nehru (1889-1964) in his book *Discovery of India* (1946), after elaborately discussing the phenomenon of 'Synthesis and Growth of Mixed Culture' observed that "...and an attempt was even made to bring about a synthesis between the religious faiths of the Hindus and the Muslims......Out of this ferment arose new types of reformers who deliberateyl preached this synthesis...In the north there was Guru Nanak."[7] He also referred to Kabir in the same breath. I shall drop Kabir as a subject of analysis for the simple reason that as compared to the Sikhs, the *Kabirpanthis*—followers of Kabir—hardly have any political identity, and are exercising much less invigorating influence on the life of Indian people. Moreover, *Kabirbāṇi*, when included in *Ādi Granth*, the scripture of tha Sikhs, forms an integral part of the Sikh tradition. And, Nehru was not alone in pursuing the course of thinking, attended by the risk of over-simplification. "The Mission of Nanak", writes Tara Chand (1888-1973) in his book *Influence of Islam on Indian Culture* (written in 1922) "was the unification of the Hindu and Musalman."[8] Yusuf Husain the author of *Glimpses of Medieval Indian Culture* (a collection of series of five lectures delivered at the University of Madras in 1954 and first time published in the year 1957) is of the view that he [Nanak] believed in the unity of God and desired to smooth the differences between Hinduism and Islam,"[9] Humayun Kabir (1906-1969) in one of the chapters entitled "Medieval Reconciliations" of his book *Indian Heritage* (delivered as Maharaj Sayaji Rao Golden Jubilee Lectures in 1943 and first time published in 1946 under the title *Our Heritage*) comes to the conclusion that "the real history of medieval India in the middle ages is thus the record of attempt at synthesis and co-operation between Hindus and Muslims."[10] The name of Nanak, besides Kabir and others, in support of his contention, readily comes to his mind.

There are also scholars like John Clark Archer, whose plan in his book *The Sikhs in Relation to Hindus, Muslims, Christians and Ahamadiyyas* (1946) is to "explain Sikhism as a venture in the reconciliation of religions."[11] Some of the Sikh scholars such as Sher Singh and Surinder Singh Kohli also subscribe to the views of synthesis. Sher Singh in *Philosophy of Sikhism* (1944) describes "Sikhism to be a distinct faith that synthesizes the best of the Indian and the Semitic traditions.[12] And, Sikhism in the opinion of Kohli, "is neither a sect of Hinduism nor of Islam. It is synthetic in character and accepts the good points of both."[13] Estlin Carpenter seems to add little more to the general hypothesis of synthesis when in *Theism in Medieval India* (1921) he states :

> The religion of Nanak, which culminated in the formation of a kind of Church Nation, was fed from two sources and attempted to establish a religion combining the higher elements of Hinduism and Islam alike.[14]

Sikhism, in the words of Arnold Joseph Toynbee (1889-1975) resolved "historic Hindu-Muslim discord."[15] Frederic Pincott while acknowledging Sikhism as a resultant of "compromise between Hinduism and Muhammedanism" points to, in his entry on Sikhism in *Hughes Dictionary of Islam* yet to another dimension of compromise when he writes that, "if it may not even be spoken of as the religion of a Muhammedan Sect."[16] Whether Sikhism is adventurous or not this is yet to be seen, but some of the scholars of Sikhism are decidely adventurous in their outlook. Those scholars who studied and evaluated teachings of Guru Nanak or the Sikh tradition in the background of Hinduism and Islam and worked out the theory of reconciliation between the two, solely relied upon the formal expressions and complascently ignored the substance contained therein. To say that the Sikh tradition is a result of compromise between Hinduism and Islam is to observe the entire phenomenon at a superficial level and thus avoiding to see things as they are.

The scholars who formulated their views about Sikhism in the background of Hinduism and Islam made use of these words as commonplaces or stock expressions thus, failing to draw a distinction between Hinduism, say of Kabir and *Brāhmaṇa* and similarly between Islam of Farid and *Qāzi.* Hinduism of *Brāhmaṇa* and Islam as interpreted by *Qāzi,* both can be termed as State Religions as they served the interests of State. Whereas, Hinduism of Kabir and Islam of Farid, both can be aptly described as Religions of the People. Those who adhere to the views of compromise, at least, agree that there arose a problem and the Sikh tradition attempted to solve it. "Mankind" writes Karl Marx (1818-1883) "always takes upon only such problem as it can solve. Since, looking at the matter more closely, we will always find that the problem itself arises only when the material conditions necessary for its solution already exist or atleast in the process of formation."[17] So the origin of the Sikh tradition in the hands of Guru Nanak, had its roots in the material conditions and it was not a compromise worked out by few individuals. Moreover, it is hard to imagine a movement of compromising nature developing into an armed revolt against the State.

Now, what were the *material* conditions which gave birth to the Sikh tradition ? The question can be answered while, to begin with, identifying Guru Nanak not as a reformer, as host of scholars contended, but as a revolutionary. "Guru Nanak" states Indubhushan Banerjee in his monumental work *The Evolution of Khalsa* (1936, 1947) "was not a reformer",[18] "he was a revolutionary"[19] "who aimed at upsetting the cherished institutions of the society in which he was born"[20] and "his object was to cut himself adrift from the old moorings and set up an independent path by itself."[21] This (according to Banerjee) seems to be the trend, in vogue. When Indubhushan Banerjee quite vehemently stressed his point to negate the views "that Guru Nanak was not a reformer; he was a revolutionary", the former was led astray as he was looking at Sikh movement mere as a historian unconcerned about the revolutionary change at the psychic level. Like a number of other scholars of Sikhism Indubhushan Banerjee also failed to assess, independently, the radical change that occurred in the process. Men and not things bring revolutions. This revolution was affected at the level of consciousness. In brief, using Sikh terminology, the *manmukh*, the degenerated being, was transformed into *gurmukh* (man of Wisdom) and both differ from each other, qualitatively. This qualitative difference lies between their motivations directly contrary to each other. The *manmukh* is endowed with dark passions *e. g. kāma* (lust), *karodha* (anger), *lobha* (greed), *Moha* (clinging) and *ahaṁkār* (ego) etc. whereas, the *gurmukh* is blessed with the virtues (or noble passions) of *sat* (truth), *santokh* (contentment), *dayā* (compassion) and *Giān* (Wisdom). It is this *gurmukh*, who, at a later stage of development of the Sikh tradition, in the hands of Guru Gobind Singh, was converted and deified as *Khālsā* and using Max Weber's expression submitted "to the ideal of uncompromising religious warfare"[22] so as to establish 'Church Nation.'

Guru Nanak launched a protest, mainly against the *Brāhmaṇical* trends of his own times and was occasionally critical about Muslim practices, then prevailing, and worked out, as a protagonist of the theory of cultural synthesis, a compromise between Hinduism and Islam. This theory does explain the origin of Sikh religion when viewed historically at a surface level. But, when we go deeper we find that the 'protest' itself was a result of some higher *Experience* of transcendental nature that transformed the psyche of its founder.

An account of 'transcendental transformation' of Nanak is recorded in *Puratan Janam Skahi* under the caption *Vain Nadi Praveś* (Entering into Vain River).[23]

The process of 'transcendental transfornation' is, also systematically worked out by Guru Nanak in *Panja Khanda* which form the part of *Japji.*[24] In the absence of such transformation of Being the 'protest' in the name of religion hardly means anything more than politics that has to operate within the power-structure in a given set of circumstances. Especially Nehru and other historians of medieval Indian culture while fitting Nanak (or Sikhism) in the general framework of their theory of 'Cultural Synthesis' were playing politices, of course, to serve the interests of Indian Nation struggling for political independence against the British Masters. The British Masters in order to instil hatred in the hearts and minds of Hindus directed against the contemporary Muslims made use of chronicles and commissioned Elliot and Dowson to translate and edit the court chronicles in such a manner that would, ultimately, drive Indians to "hail the British regime as blessing."[25] Nehru's and his fellow-travellers's attempt in the given set of circumstances, was laudable. But, at the same time it is also true that they *inadvertently* sacrificed the higher truth contained in the teachings of Guru Nanak. The higher truth, in the instant case, is that every religious discipline, termed as Path, and as delineated by the respective founders of religion, (and not the followers of religion), is unique and complete unto itself, not only leads to the Ultimate Goal of life, but also in the process converts an ordinary person into a Vibrant Being, full of Compassion. It was in this background that Guru Nanak advised Muslim to be true Muslim. Realizing, that it is difficult, indeed, to follow the instructions of the founder in their unmixed form. Guru Nanak addresses the Muslim, thus :

Musalmān Kahāvana muskala
Jañ hoi tañ Musalmāna Kāhāve
Awal owl dīna kara miṭhā
Maskala mānā māla musāve
Hoi Muslim dīna muhāne
Maraṇa jīwan kā bharma cukāve
Rabb ki rajāe mane, sir ūpara kartā mane
Āpa gavāve
Tau Nanak sarab jia mein rehmata hoi
tañ Musalmāna kahāve-[26]

When paraphrased it means that in order to be a true Muslim, difficult indeed it is, one should cherish faith in *Allāh*; and with this he should scrap the rust of ego, should take lead in preaching and practising the faith: and shed away the illusion of Life and Death; ought to submit to the Will of God and thus dissolve his ego and is Compassionate to living beings.

Similarly, Guru Nanak desired to restore the original definition of *Brāhmaṇa* when he says :

"*So Brāhmana jo brahama bicāre.*"[27]
Āpa tare sagle kul tāre

Only he is *Brahmaṇa* who has realized *Brahma*.

Not only that he transcends the ocean of existence himslf. But also helps others.

By implications he expects Sikhs to be true Sikhs and presented before them the ideal of *gurmukh*.

Ramakrishna Paramhaṁsa (1836-1886)[28] in modern times, pursuing an experiential approach to the study of religion made experiments with the religions such as Islam and Christianity, and following the Paths realized the same Goal.

To attempt a synthesis of religions only means to dilute them.

Max Arthur Macauliffe (1837-1913) in the Preface to his book *The Sikh Religion* (1909) has expressed views contrary to the views of those scholars of Sikh tradition, who in one way or the other, categorized it as derivative. In a declarative tone Macauliffe writes, that :

> Now, there is here presented a religion totally unaffected by Semitic or Christian influence. Based on the concept of the unity of God it rejected Hindu formularies and adopted an independent ethical system, ritual and standards which were totally opposed to the theolgical beliefs of Guru Nanak's age and country. As we shall see hereafter, it would be difficult to point to a religion of greater originality or to a more comprehensive ethical system.[29]

Indubhushan Banerjee, in a way, was undermining the views of Macauliffe when the former, unapproringly, states that "his [Nanak] object was to cut himself adrift from the old moorings and set up an independent path by itself.[30] Macauliffe, while describing Sikhism as a revolt against Hinduism has only referred to its rejection of Hindu formularies. His enthusiasm to establish Sikhism as absolutely original was not devoid of motives. "One of the main objects of the present work [*The Sikh Religion*]" discloses Macauliffe, "is to endeavour to make some reparation to the Sikhs for the insult which he [Ernest Trumpp] offered to their Gurus and their religion."[31] Other things apart Macauliffc was indirectly referring to the following comments of Trumpp which the latter offered with regard to *Ādi Granth* :

> (i) ....By thus jumbling together whatever came to hand without any judicious selection the

Granth has become an extremely incoherent and wearisome book......

(ii) ....Though the *Granth* as regards its contents is perhaps the most shallow and empty book that exists in proportion to its size.[32]

Macauliffe as a scholar was certainly serving the interests of British Masters who not only wanted to create a gulf between the Hindus and the Sikhs but also were interested '*to win over the*' Sikhs.

To be an original means to raise an original question. Guru Nanak, the Founder—Guru of Sikh religion did raise a question, and an original one. Originality does not lie in asking a question which is absolutely new and unheard of, as 'there is nothing new under the Sun.' It means to strive to reach the origin of the predicament of human life. Thus, an original is not opposed to an old; it is opposed to what is superficial. It also means to respond to the totality of circumstances that helps to evolve an integrated view of life. In fact, it is hang-together of different constituents, already available, that makes any thing or idea original. The original question, in this sense, that Guru Nanak raised was :

Kiva Saciārā Hoiai ?[33]

How to *become* (embodiment of) Truth ? The said question is repeated, but, in different form thus :

Kiva Kūṛai tuṭai pāl (*i*) ?[34]

How can (one) transcend the limits of Untruth ? Thus, (*Saca*) and Untruth (*Kūṛa*) are juxtaposed to each other as antonym. Guru Nanak also answered the question, in the same breath, saying :

Hukam (i) *rajāi calaṇā Nānak likhiyānāl* (*i*)[35]

By living in accordance with Law that is writ alongwith. The fundamental question, here, is that of mode of Being. In other words, how to effect a transformation of Being—from Untruth to Truth ? Moreover, such a transformation results in having a different quality of Being. This is possible, as revealed by Guru Nanak, while living in accordance with the Law which is inherently written alongwith one's Being. This Law is Universal. The instant effect of the realization of this Universal Law on human psyche, in the words of Guru Nanak is :

Nānak hukamai Je bujhai
ta hō(u) maī kahaī nā koe...[36]
Whosoever lives according to the Law
Shall not indulge in Ego.

That one transcends the limits of Ego. Here, Hukam (*Law*) and *Hō(u)mui* (Ego) are placed said by side, as antonym. Now we have two pairs of opposites : Truth (*Saca*), Untruth (*Kūṛa*) and Law (*Hukam*)—Ego ((*Hō*(*u*) *mai*). To sum up : Law leads one to Truth and Ego to Uutruth. Again, those who imbibe Truth, in *Gurbāṇi* are termed as *Gurmukh* opposed to *Manmukh*, the latter soaked up with Untruth. Since, *Gurmukh* and *Manmukh* are different from each other—different in their quality of Beings—so, they are to be judged, only from their *amal* or mode of behaviour and they do behave not only differently but contrarily. The mode of behaviour of *Gurmukh* is guided by the virtues of *Saca* (Truth), *Santokh* (contentment) *Dayā* (compassion) and *Giān* (Wisdom). In fact, these are the manifestations which stem from the state of 'No Mind' which is not absence of mind, at all. When put differently these virtues are the result of purified state of (mind). What renders mind impure ? The answer is that it is Ego that renders mind impure. The impurities of mind consist of, to enlist only a few, *Kāma* (Lust) *Karodha* (Anger), *Lobha* (Greed), *Moha* (Ignorance) and *Ahaṁkāra* (Ego) etc. And, one who embodies these vices, in the language of *Gurbāṇi*, is looked down upon as *Manmukh*.

Guru Nanak put forth an Ideal of *Gurmukh* before the humanity. He criticised the prevailing religious practices of say, *Brāhmanism*,[37] *Jainism*[38] and *Islam*[39] etc., also expressed his views pertaining to political developments.[40] and condemned the functionaries of contemporary feudal set-up on the ground of their mal-functioning, contrary to the demands of truth and justice, but with reference to the model of religion hc presented for the spiritual well-being of man and woman, both. Woman in its ideal form, in *Gurbāṇi*, is identified as *Suhāgaṇ* (intune with God). Man and woman, in fact, masculinity and femininity, these are two major expressions of Cosmic Reality.

One is born out of unison of man and woman. As a result of that, in the innermost core of Being, there dwell both man and woman, in some proportion, that creates bisexuality within. Every human being is bisexual in the sense that it combines both the masculine and feminine irrespective of being a man or woman. This psychological truth was discovered in India, long ago, and projected in the myth of *ardhanāriśvara*.[41]

The fact of human beings imbibing composite psychic nature is also acknowledged by Guru Nanak himself when he says, that :

> There is a woman in man
> and man in woman.
> Only wise can discern it.[42]

Bisexuality as a psychic phenomenon, is a subject of study in modern psychology, too. "Every individual..............." discovered Sigmund Freud (1856-1939) "displays a mixture of the character-traits belonging to his own and to the opposite sex, and he shows a combination of activity and passivity whether or not these last character-traits tally with his biological ones."[43] Freud identified activity in woman as a masculine trait and passivity in man as a feminine one. And, passivity, as such, might have its roots in male-dominant society. Anyhow, psychologically speaking, every individual is to be viewed in this backgrovnd. Therefore, both the masculine and feminine tendencies operate within one and the same individual being. To emphasize upon these tendencies is not to overlook the difference between male and female biological organism. Rather, the purpose is to keep oneself aware of the subtle distinctions that effect one's entire mode of behaviour. It is this awareness that unfolds the mystery as to why Guru Nanak and other Gurus of the Sikhs and medieval Indian saints like Kabir display their feminine psychic Being while expressing their *premā-bhakti* or devovion towards *Īśvara.* And, *suhāgaṇ* is one who has been blessed with the unison with *Īśvara. Duhāgaṇa,* on the other hand, is one who continues to be deprived of such a blessing of *Īśvara. Suhāgāṇa* and *Duhāgaṇa,* therefore, are the feminine counterparts of *Gurmukh* and *Manmukh,* respectively. Unlike in Jainism and (Theravāda) Buddhism, which are, (as opposed to devotion) meditative in their religious discipline can accomodate, only masculinity, whereas, in Sikhism masculinity and femininity, both can work out their *mokśa.* Meditation is conducive for masculine Being and femininity longs only for devotion. Sikhism provides two different Paths of meditation and devotion to two different modes of masculine and feminine behaviour.

It was Compassion for the people that impelled Guru Nanak to undertake Travels called *Udasis* so as to drive them out from their ignorance, which is not an error of intellect, as generally construed, but a spiritual blindness. Guru Nanak wanted that his message of Compassion should take a concrete shape. He "started building new institutions, such as a Church, without priestcraft which he named *saṅgat*, a community kitchen open to man of all castes and creeds known to this day as *laṅgar*."[44] Both these institutions helped in inculcating feeling of fraternity among the people. Another very significant thing that Guru Nanak brought into being was *bāṇi pothi* that contained his own hymns and that of others like Farid and Kabir, saturated with the ultimate message of Compassion for suffering humanity.

Guru Nanak appointed Guru Aṅgad (1504-1552) as his successor. Guru Aṅgad continued preaching the model of religion of Guru Nanak, adding few things more that helped the religion in emerging as an institution. Two things, in this context, deserve special mention. Guru Aṅgad gave special attention to *laṅgar* (community kitchen). Thus inter-dining helped in developing good feeling among the people and, gradually, casting off the caste-distinctions. Another thing, having far-reaching effects, the Guru did was to give shape to *Gurmukhi* script. Guru Nanak had handed over a *bāṇi-pothi* to Guru Aṅgad that also contained his own hymns, besides that of other Saints, naturally, in written form. This collection also contained a *Paṭṭi.*[45] (acrostic) consisting of thirty-five letters. Guru Aṅgad studied and modified the script of the *Paṭṭi* and gave it the name of *Gurmukhi*. Now the Sikhs had their own language with distinct script.

Guru Amar Das (1479-1574) succeeded Guru Aṅgad. *Laṅgar*, in the hands of Guru Amar Das, became an institution and anybody desiring to meet the Guru had first to take meals in *laṅgar*. Even, Akbar, the Mughal Emperor, when visited the Guru, had to take meals in *laṅgar*, before he was allowed to meet the Guru.

The Guru, also to facilitate the collection of offerings made by the Sikhs reorganized his area of influence into twenty two *manjis* or parishes under the control of *masaṅds*. Here, it may be quite significant to point out that the Mughal Empire during the reign of Akbar (r. 1556-1605) was also divided into the same number of *parganās*.

Guru Amar Das adopted certain measures which resulted in providing impetus to the Sikhs in establishing the identity of their own. The ceremonies regarding births and deaths of the Sikhs were given new orientation. Sanskrit *Ślokās* were dispensed with and replaced by the hymns of the Gurus. This, certainly, minimised the role of *Brahmaṇa*, in day to day living. Initiating the process of remarriage of widows and abolition of the practice of *Sati* by Guru Amar Das, turned the *Brahāmaṇas* hostile to the Guru and his Sikhs.

Guru Amar Das passed on his holy ministry to Guru Ram Das (1534-1581) who built the town of Ram Das Pura, (later on known as Amritsar), invited traders to settle down there. He sent Bhai Gurdas (1543/1553-1637) the first Sikh preacher to Agra, to preach the religion of Guru Nanak, outside the Panjab. The Sikh movement in the hands of Guru Ram Das further got expanded and acquired dimensions political in nature.

The fourth Guru, Guru Ram Das transferred his spiritual powers to Guru Arjan (1563-1606). The Sikh tradition in the times of Guru Arjan, not only acquired peculiar dimensions, having far-reaching results but also got crystalised. The Guru built *Harimandir Sahib*, on a foundation-stone laid by Mian Mir the (Muslim) Saint of Lahore. To raise money required for the completion of *Harimandir Sahib*, the Guru introduced a system of *dasvandh* i. e. one tenth of the income, obligatory for every Sikh to contribute for the cause, through the *masaṇds* to be deposited with the Guru on the day of *Baisākhi*, every year. Guru Arjan also raised the cities of Taran Taran near Amritsar and Kartarpur in the District of Jullundhur besides Sri Hargobindpur, built on the bank of river Beas.

The most significant task that Guru Arjan accomplished was the compilation of Ādi Granth, which made the Sikh religion a Religion of the Book. But it was the martyrdom of Guru Arjan during the reign of Mughal Emperor, Jahangir (r. 1605-1626) in 1606 that brought about a qualitative change in the character of Sikh movement. There might have been number of domestic and/or social reasons that worked against Guru Arjan but the paramount consideration, no doubt, was of political nature. Emperor Jahangīr has himself recorded his annoyance in his diary *Tuzuk-e-Jahangiri*, over the activities of Guru Arjan, in the words—

> ....At last when Khusrau [Jahangir's son] passed along this road this insignificant fellow [Guru Arjan] proposed to wait upon him. Khusrau happened to halt at the place where he was, and he came out and did homage to him. He behaved to Khusrau in certain special ways and made on his forehead a finger-mark in saffron, which the Indians call *qaśqā* [*tilak*] and is considered to be propitious. So many of the simple-minded Hindus, nay, many foolish Muslims too, had been fascinated by his ways and teachings. He was noised about as a religious and worldly leader. They called him Guru and from all directions crowds of fools would come to him and express great devotion to him. This busy traffic had been carried on for three or four generations. For

> years the thought had been presenting itself to my mind that either I should put an end to this false traffic, or he should be brought into the fold of Islam.[46]

A careful scrutiny of the above passage would lead to no other conclusion than that Emperor Jahangir's assessment, that too coupled with irritable expressions, was absolutely correct that Guru Arjan had become a force to reckon with. If we look into the gradually increasing emphasis on Guru the Person[47] (as opposed to Guru the Principle) we can say that it was a deliberate attempt on the part of the Gurus to acquire a significance of symbol of unity for the Sikhs. It was this unity that could be a challenge for any existing monarchy. The martyrdom of Guru Arjan, therefore, was a result of clash between the Mughal monarcy and the Sikh Church.

Guru Hargobind (1595-1644), son of Guru Arjan and successor to *Gurgaddi*, in view of martyrdom of the latter took to arms in a regular way. He wore two swords of (i) *mīrī* symbolizing temporal power and (ii) *pīrī* signifying spiritual power and also added an emblem of royalty tied on his turban. In order to further specify the changed character of the Sikh movement Guru Hargobind built a fortress called Lohgarh in Amritsar. The raising of *Akāl Takht* in the vicinity of *Harimandir Sahib* was another significant step in giving militant character to the Sikh movement. The Guru while sitting on *Akāl Takhat* administered justice. The Guru told the Sikhs, writes Khazan Singh in his book *History of the Sikh Religion* (1914) "that as long as he continued in *Harimandir Sahib* he should be looked upon as a Saint and in the *Akāl Buṅgā* he should be looked upon as a king."[47] Thus the Sikh religion and Sikh politics was integrated forming a one whole in the person of Guru called *Sacā Pādśāh*.

Describing the style of functioning of Guru Hargobind, Khushwant Singh writes :

> The Guru's abode did in fact become like that of the Emperor. He sat on a throne and held court. He went out with a royal umbrella over his head and was always accompanied by armed retainers. He sent envoys to ruling princes and received their agents in durbar, where presents were exchanged. With Arjan the title *Sacā Pādśāh* was only honorific, with Hargobind it became a reality as far as the Sikhs were concerned. He was *mirī pirī dā mālik* (the lord of the spiritual and secular domains).[48]

There is yet one more very significant dimension of 'Guru Hargobind sitting on a throne' and which has been very aptly described by Trilochan Singh in the words that,

> The very erection of *Akāl-Takhat* (Throne of the Almighty) was a challenge to all coercive authority of the Mughal Emperors, an assertion of super national autonomy, and of freedom from all fear and despotic rule. Near the *Akāl-Takhat* flew his flag of freedom.[49]

On wearing two swords of *mirī* and *pirī* by Guru Hargobind, Gopal Singh has a novel idea to put forth. He is of the view that "the unwary interpret it as the Guru's desire to combine religion with politics !"[50] Gopal Singh has made futile attempt to work out his thesis of comparatmentalization of life and pursued the course of adhering to the dichotomy of religion and politics which is contrary to the Sikh *Weltanschaung* and which is unitary in nature. Gopal Singh's interpretation of *mirī* and *pirī* seems to have stemed from his *loyalities*.

The Mughal monarchy at the Centre could hardly afford to overlook these developments aimed at to defy its authority. The interested parties instigated Emperor Jahangir and the latter under the pretext of the fine imposed on Guru Arjan not having been paid so far, put Hargobind, as a prisoner, in the fort of Gwalior (Circa 1609). The Guru was detained for about one year and after his release he again took up the task, now more vigorously, of consolidating his position as a Rebel against the State. This could not be possible without raising an army and which he did. Besides that the Guru, in order to give impetus to the Sikh movement, personally, undertook tour of Uttar Pradesh and Kashmir and created followers imbibing missionary zeal tempered with martial spirit. And Guru Hargobind did clash with the 'coercive, authority of the Mughal Emperor' number of times. In fact, these clashes came more prominently on surface during the reign of Shahjahan (r. 1628-1658) who after the death of Jahangir in 1627 was crowned as a new Emperor. Guru Hargobind, accordiag to Kishan Singh,[51] as a matter of strategy, did not, deliberately, entered into conflict with Emperor Jahangir, so as to build up a Sikh movement as a force to reckon with, however, without diluting the revolutionary contents of the movement. First time Shahjahan and Guru Hargobind clashed with each other in 1628, the year Shahjahan occupied the throne of Mughal Empire, over a issue that may be referred to as a 'hawk and duck dispute.' It so happened that the hawk of Shahjahan while chasing a duck entered the Guru's camp. The Guru also, in order to capture the duck, flew his hawk. In this pursuit the Sikhs seized both the duck and the Emperor's hawk. Refusal on the part of the Sikhs to return hawk made Emperor, who was staying at Lahore, to deploy Mukhlis Khan, the Army General to arrest the Guru and bring back the hawk. In this battle that was fought at the outskirts of Amritsar the Guru defeated the Mughal army.

Again in 1631 the Guru and the Mughal army confronted each other over the issue of horses. The *masands* of Kabul had brought two horses to be presented to the Guru as *nazrānā* (gift) and which were snatched away by the Mughal officials and thus presented to Shahjahan. The Guru deputed Bidi Chand, his devotee, to rescue the horses and he accomplished the assigned task diligently. This naturally enraged the Emperor and he despatched force under the command of Lala Beg to enforce submission of the Guru to the imperial authority Both the armies met at Gurusar in district Nabha and in this battle though both the sides suffered heavily, ultimately the Guru once again emerged victorious.

The issues over which the Guru clashed with Mughal monarchy were certainly of trivial nature, but underlying idea was certainly in no way other than to defy the Mughal authority.

Summing up the developments of the Sikh movement till the times of Guru Hargobind, Joseph Davey Cunningham writes :

> During the ministry of Hargobind, the Sikhs increased greatly in number, and fiscal policy of Arjun and the armed system of his son, had already formed them into a kind of separate State within the Empire.[52]

After the death of Guru Hargobind in 1644, Har Rai (1630-1661), the younger son of the Guru's eldest son Baba Gurdita, became the seventh Guru of the Sikhs. The Guru was quite friendly with Dara Shikoh, the son of Shahjahan, Guru Har Rai supported Dara Shikoh who lost the war. The victorious Aurangzeb asked Guru Har Rai as to why did he lend his (moral) support to Dara Shikoh. The Guru sent his son Ram Rai to Delhi, who through his sycophancy[53] won over the confidence of the Emperor Aurangzeb. Excepting this clash, not altogether without political overtones with the Mughal monarchy, there is nothing on record to show that the Guru continued with the rebellious spirit he had inherited from the predecessor-Gurus, especially, Guru Hargobind who was militant in his disposition.

Guru Har Rai installed his younger son Hari Krishan (1656-1664), as his successor in 1661 the year he died. It is believed that at the instance of *masands* Aurangzeb called Guru Hari Krishan to Delhi, desiring to decide the issue of claim of *Gurgaddi* between him and his elder brother Ram Rai. Guru Hari Krishan came to Delhi and before he died of small-pox, categorically stated denouncing the claim of both Dhir Mal and Ram Rai and referred to his successor living at Bakala, district Amritsar. The Guru at the time of his death, uttered only the words 'Baba Bakale' meaning thereby that the next Guru was at Bakala. But, as this indication did not categorically point out as to the identity of the Successor-Guru "nearly twenty-two pretenders set themselves up as successor to Guru Hari Krishan at Bakala."[54] And, it was Makhan Shah Labaṇa, a trader who exposed the pretenders and convincingly established the fact that it was Guru Tegh Bahadur and, none else, who was referred to as Baba Bakale.[55] Now Guru Tegh Bahadur (1621-1675) was the rightful ninth Guru of the Sikhs.

The Sikh Gurus and Mughal monarchs had started interfering with each other's affairs.

The most important thing for us, at present, is to look into the circumstances which turned Guru Tegh Bahadur Rebel against the State. Aurangzeb (r. 1658-1707) desired "unstinted political loyalty from the whole country"[56] so as "to build the totalitarian State of his dream"[57] and he was made to believe that it could be possible only, if the *Brāhmins* were eliminated. And, in the absence of this priestly class Hinduism *must* wither away. As a follow up action the

Brāhmins were put into prisons, thus, made victim by coercive measures to ensure their conversion into the Religion of the Ruler. It was during this crisis that Pandit Kirpa Ram, leading a deputation of the *Brāhmins* of all shades went to Anandpur Sahib and approached Guru Teg Bahadur for help. After due deliberations Guru Tegh Bahadur told Pandit Kirpa Ram, to convey it to Aurangzeb that "if he succeeds in converting Tegh Bahadur then all *Brāhmins* and there after the Hindus of the whole country would accept Islam."[58] The Guru proceeded to Agra to meet Aurangzeb, there. He was arrested alongwith his four companions[59] and taken to Delhi by the Mughal officials because Aurangzeb, meanwhile, had moved to Delhi. Aurangzeb tried but failed in his mission to convert Guru Tegh Bahadur to Islam and as a result of that the Guru was beheaded on November 11, 1675 in Chandni Chowk, Delhi.

The martyrdom of Guru Tegh Bahadur was a result of hostility against the State combined with Compassion even for those who adhered to different model of religion.[60]

Before Guru Tegh Bahadur died as martyr he passed on *Gurgaddi* to his son Gobind Rai, later known as Guru Gobind Singh (1666-1708). The Guru successfully fought the battle of Bhangani against the Rajputs in 1686 and led the Hussaini Yudh in 1687 against the Mughals besides building fortresses such as Anandgarh, Keshgarh, Lohgarh and Fatehgarh. But most significant contribution of Guru Gobind Singh, the tenth Guru of Sikhs, to the Sikh movement was the creation of *Khālsā*. The Guru's decision to evolve an Order of *Khālsā* was not suddenly arrived at but a culmination of the Sikh movement. The Gurus, hitherto, have been resisting the capriciousness and the tyranny of the Rulers while adhering to the precept of non-violence. Nevertheless, the Gurus felt the need of the force, kept it also and made use of it in self-defence. Especially, Guru Hargobind after the martyrdom of Guru Arjan, on the advice of the latter, raised an army and Guru Har Rai maintained it for the said purpose. The martyrdom of Guru Arjan and Guru Tegh Bahadur was also in the back of the Guru's mind. So, it was a high time to organize an armed revolt against the State administered by an Emperor like Aurangzeb, who was determined 'to convert *dar-al-harb* (land of infidelity) into *dar-al-Islam* (land of faith).

It is generally agreed[61] that the birth of *Khālsā* commenced on March 30, 1699 at Anandpur. Imagine ! the Guru appearing before the congregation (*Saṅgat*), carrying a naked sword in his hand and roaring like a lion, asks for the head. There is a perfect stillness for a while. The Guru repeats his demand thrice. Then Bhai Daya Ram Sobti is escorted to a nearby enclosure. The Guru again asks for a second head. Now Dharam Das offers his head. But, the Guru is not satisfied with just two; he needs more heads. Thereafter, Mohkam Chand, Sahib Chand and Himmat Rai came forward, one after the other. All the five were taken into an enclosure, one by one, but, were brought back, simultaneously, dressed in a uniform. The congregation rejoiced and welcomed them with the utterance of *Sat Siri Akāl.* These five, who willingly offered their heads to the Guru for upholding the tenets of *dharma*, go into the annals of the Sikh history as *Pañj Pyāre.* They were administered *amrit* (nectar) prepared by Guru himself.[62] It was not all over. Now the Guru asked the *Pañj Pyāres* to baptize him in the same manner. A good number of Sikhs were, thus, admitted into a new order on that day, which gradually increased and became a force to reckon with.

The Guru, in order to make the *Khālsā* a diciplined soldier, made it obligatory to observe five *K's*, (K is one of the alphabets of the *Gurmukhi* script) and these are : i. *keś* (unshorn hair); ii. *kirpān* (sword), iii. *kaṅghā* (comb); iv *karā* (steel bracelet) and v. *kacchā* (underwear). Besides that the Guru instructed the male *Khālsā* to use *Singh* and the female *Khālsā* to add *Kaur* as an appellation. Equally important was the understanding given to the new convert that henceforth entry into a new order amounts to – *kritnāś* (previous occupations); ii. *kulnāś* (family ties); iii. *dharmanāś* (earlier creeds) and *karmanāś* (rituals) thus enabling him to live upto the norms of a new fraternity.[63]

There is hardly any need to stress the point that the *Khālsā* was absolutely distinct from the contemporary Hindu brethren both in appearance and ideal.

After the creation of the *Khālsā* the character of the Sikh community is said to have altogether changed. As, "the bulk of the converts were Jat peasants of the central districts of the Panjab,"[64] the rise of militant Sikhism" in the words of Khushwant Singh, "became the rise of Jat power in the Panjab."[65] And, armed revolt, in fact, was the revolt of peasantry which was also, later on spearheaded by Banda Bahadur. Jagjit Singh holds a different view. "The armed struggle" according to him, "was not based on clannish, tribal, feudal or dynastic loyalities or ambitions either."[66] Agreed, that "the only tribes from which a sizable number of Sikhs were drawn were the Jats. But, as they shed off their Jatism when they joined the *Khālsā*, the question of their original clannish and tribal ties did not arise."[67]

It was in this very context of joining the Order of *Khālsā* that the phenomena of *krītnāś*, *kulnāś*, *dharmanāś* and *karmanāś* became a reality.

In view of the rebellious spirit of the *Khālsā*, the lines *Rāj kare gā Khālsā* (the *Khālsā* shall rule) need to be understood in proper perspective These lines occur in the *Tankhwah-Namah* of Bhai Nand Lal (1633-1705) who was a devotee and court poet of Guru Gobind Singh. The full couplet, that forms the part of recitation after the *ardās*, reads :

> *Rāj karegā Khālsā, yāqī raheī na koe,*
> *Khwar hoe sabh milenge bace sarn jo hoe,*[68]
> The *Khālsā* shall rule, none opposed to him shall exist.
> Dejected they shall surrender, and those seeking refuge shall be saved.

The key-word, of course, in the above couplet is *Khālsā.* There is a widespread tendency to translate the word *Khālsā* into English as 'pure' and which is not at all a correct equivalent of the word *Khālsā.* Ganda Singh, a great Sikh historian, while clarifying the misinterpretation states that :

> It is not always correct, particularly in the context of this couplet, to translate the word *Khālsā* as 'pure'. The word for pure is *Khālis.* Derived, of course, from *Khālis, Khālsā* is, in fact a technical term which in the days of Mughal administration meant inalienable lands of revenues directly looked after or administered by the Government or the King. Guru Gobind Singh applied this word specifically to those of the Sikhs whom he had baptized as *Singhs,* the Lions.[69]

The Guru, therefore, used the word *Khālsā* by way of analogy. The analogous use of the word *Khālsā* becomes amply clear when we look into the greeting that reads, thus :

> *Vah Gurū Ji Kā Khālsā*
> *Vah Gurū Jī Kī Fateh.*
> The Khālsā belongs to God
> And so does the victory.

The analogy is : that *Khālsā* belongs to God the way *Khālsā* land belongs to king. The Guru created *Khālsā* to wage a *dharma yudh* to destroy the evil as commanded by God Himself. [70]

The couplet *Rāj karegā Khālsā* came into vogue during the times of Banda Singa Bahadur (1710-1716) in order to seek moral force against the measures of persecution adopted by the Mughal Emperors to eliminate the community.

The Order of *Khālsā* naturally made the hill-chiefs all around apprehensive and they joined hands against the Guru, under the leadership of Raja of Bilaspur. The hill-chiefs created number of difficulties for the Guru.

The Guru moved from Anandpur to Nirmoh near Kiratpur. Even that did not satisfy the hill-chiefs and they managed help from Mughal forces and made a joint attack on the Guru. They did not succeed in their plan, however, the Guru left for Basali. At a later stage, the hill-chiefs compromised with the Guru.

The compromise between the hill-chiefs and the Guru could not and did not last long as the latter wanted them to own the ideal of *Khālsā.* One thing is amply clear that Guru Gobind Singh was not a feudal *Rājā* like Rājās of the hill. In fact, the hill-chiefs were feeling demoralized in the face of valour of the *Khālsā* and wanted to destroy them in order to ensure their own existence. In such circumstances, it is not at all difficult to muster help from the Centre. They instigated Aurangzeb, the Mughal Emperor, against the Guru and with the help of Mughal forces besieged Anandpur which continued for some time. The Guru evacuated Anandpur as a result of deal against the promise made by the Mughals not to harm him on the way, and which they did not keep up. The Mughal forces attacked the Guru on the way, but he succeeded in arriving at Chamakaur. The Mughal army besieged Chamakaur. In this battle, two sons of the Guru—Ajit Singh and Jujhar Singh besides a good numebr of *Khālsā* were killed. The Guru escaped and Mughal troops followed him but was saved by two *Paṭhans*.

After the execution of Zorawar Singh and Fateh Singh, the younger sons of Guru Gobind Singh, Wazir Khan, Sūba of Sirhind marched against the Guru staying at Kot Kapura. A pitch battle was fought between the *Khālsā* and the Mughals at the village Khidrana, where the 'famous forty' laid down their lives in the cause of *dharma* that resulted in the utter defeat of the imperial forces. The village Khidrana is now known as Mukatsar.

When Guru Gobind Singh was facing the hostilities of hill-chiefs Prince Mu'azzam had helped him in many ways and in return the Guru had also lent his support to the Prince while fighting a war of succession and there was nothing new in such a move. When the Prince became a new Mughal Emperor assuming the name of Bahadur Shah, the Guru paid him a courtesy call at Agra. When Bahadur Shah marched against his brother Kam Baksh towards Deccan the Guru also accompained him. Guru Gobind Singh at this point of time adopted the policy of Guru Hargobind had, at one time, formulated in order to rejuvenate the movement. Adjustment with each other suited both the Guru and the Emperor. The Guru took the advantage of the situation which helped him to rebuild the shattered movement.[71] The Guru stayed at Nader and it was here that Lachman Das, a hermit, (later known as Banda Singh Bahadur) met the Guru who converted him and transformed him into a valiant soldier enjoining him a 'holy mission' to establish an egalitarian State in the Panjab with instructions not to rule as a Sovereign, but as one among the *Khālsā*.

The Guru's success in his mission to rebuild the movement in the background of his friendly relations with the Emperor, was a fatal blow to the designs of Wazir Khan, Sūbā of Sirhind. To counteract, Wazir Khan sent a hired *Paṭhan* to Nader who made a fatal attack on Guru Gobind Singh who passed away there in 1708. Consequent upon that the Guru could not visit the Panjab as planned.

The rebellious spirit of the Gurus was twofold : (i) to establish an identity of their religion, separate from Hinduism (or *Brāhmanism*), outside the caste-structure and to constitute a Church Nation of their own; (ii) to combat against the coercive authority of the Mughal Emperors (or their allies) at the Centre and build-up their own State within Empire, egalitarian in character.

References and Notes

1-2. Ernest Trumpp (Trs.) *The Ādi Granth*, p. Ci (Introduction).

3. Gokul Chand Narang, *Transformation of Sikhism* p. 249.

4. Gurbachan Singh Talib, *Guru Nanak : His Personality and Vision*, p. 322.

5. W. H. Mcleod, *Guru Nanak and the Sikh Religion*, p. 160

6. Stephen Dunning, *The Sikh Religion : An Examination of some of the Western Studies in Journal of Religious Studies*. p. 20.

7. Jawaharlal Nehru, *The Discovery of India*, pp. 239-240.

8. Tara Chand, *Influence of Islam on Indian Culture* p. 168.

9. Yusuf Husain, *Glimpses of Medieval Indian Culture*, p. 29.

10. Humayun Kabir, *Indian Heritage*, p. 65.

11. John Clark Archer, *The Sikhs in Relation to Hindus, Christians and Ahmadiyyas*, p. 5.

12. Stephen Dunning *op. cit.* p. 2 also see Ref. 2, p. 23: Sher Singh, *Philosophy of Sikhism* p. 7! :
The background of Sikhism is not Hindu alone but Aryan and Semitic both.
13. Surinder Singh Kohli, *A Critical Study of Adi Granth*, pp. 370-371.
14. J. Estlin Carpenter, *Theism in Medieval India*, p. 489.
15. Arnold Toynbee, *Selections From the Sacred Writings of the Sikhs*. p. 10 (Foreword)
16. Frederic Pincott, *Dictionary of Islam*, p. 583.
17. Karl Marx and Frederick Engles, *A Contribution to the Critique of Political Economy in Selected Works*, Vol. I, p. 363.
18-21. Indubhushan Banerjee, *The Evolution of Khalsa* Vol. I, p. 113.
22. Max Weber, *The Sociology of Religion* (translated by Ephraim Fischoff) p. 88.
23. Kirpal Singh (Ed) *Janam Sakhi Prampara* pp. 8-9 (Appendix).
24. Japji, *Ādi Granth* pp. 7-8.
25. Khaliq Ahmed Nizami and Abdur Rashid (Edts.) *Elliot and Dawson's History of India*, an article, General Criticism of Elliot's Approach to Medieval Indian History (Original Vol. I, p. 22) p. 763.
26. *Ādi Granth* p. 141.
27. *Ādi Granth*. p. 662.
28. *Life of Sri Ramakrisana*, For the Practice of Muhammedan Faith see – pp. 207-208; Regarding Christ, pp. 253-255.
29. Max Arthur Macauliffe, *The Sikh Religion*, pp. iv-v (Introduction) Volume I and II combined.
30. Indubhushan Banerjee, *loc. cit.*
31. Max Arthur Macauliffe *op. cit.* Vol. I, p vii (Preface)
32. Ernest Trumpp, *op. cit.* p. cxxii; p. cxxi.

33-36. Japji : *Ādi Granth* p. 1.

37. Guru Nanak in Vār Āśā Mehallā I (Ādi Granth p. 471) condemned the wearing-in-ceremony of sacred thread (Janeū) – which was a part of *Brāhmnism*, on the ground that this ceremony hardly initiates one to imbibe the virtues of Dayā (Compassion), *santokh* (contentment), *Jat* (continence) and *Sat* (Truth).

38. Similarly, Guru Nanak was highly critical about day-to-day ritualistic performances of Jain *Sādhu*, being futile. See Vār Majh Mehllā I (Ādi Granth p. 141)

39. Again Guru Nanak in Vār Mājh Mehllā I (Ādi Granth p 141) refers to the Five Time Prayer of Muslims and pointing out its ritual characteristic provides a new orientation in the background of human virtues.

40. In *Babar Vāṇī* that consists of four verses (three in *Aśā Rāg* on pp. 360, 417 and one in *Tilang Rāg* on pp. 722-723 of Ādi Granth) concerning Babar's invasions on India (Emnabad) in 1521, Guru Nanak condemns mode of living perpetuating the system based on Māyā in favour of his own model committed to Truth.

41. *Śiva-paurāna : Satrudra Saṁhitā* See. Gopi Nath T. Rao *Elements of Hīndu Iconography* Vol. II, Part I, pp. 321-331,

42. Ādi Granth p. 879.

43. James Starchey (Gen. Ed) *The Complete Psychological Works of Sigmund Freud.* Vol. VII p, 220.

44. Trilochan Singh, *Guru Tegh Bahadur* p. 15

45. Ādi Granth pp. 432-434 (Rag Aśā Mehallā I) Also see *Paṭṭi* pp. 434-435 (Rāg Āsā Mehallā III)

46. Alexander Rogers and H. Beveridges, (Trs.) *Tuzuk-e-Jehangir-i* Vol. I. p. 72.

47. For detailed analysis sec : Harbhajan Singh, *Gurmukhi lipi Mein Hindi Kāvya* pp. 83-86.

47a. Khazan Singh, *History of the Sikh Religion* p. 130; *Gurbilas Padsahi Chaivin* :

Sant rūp hoe mainrahan Hartmandir ke mah
Rajo rūp ehthe rahan Akal Takhat sukh pāe.

48. Khushwant Singh *op. cit.* pp. 63-64. n.

49. Trilochan Singh, *Guru Tegh Bahadur, Prophet and Martyr.* p. 3.

50. Gopal Singh, *A History of the Sikh People* p. 829 (Appendix XI)

51. Kishan Singh, *Sikh Lehar* p. 45

52. Joseph Davey Cunningham, *History of Sikhs.* p. 53; Hari Ram Gupta, *History of the Sikh Gurus* p. 93

53. There occurs an expression, 'mitti musalman *ki paire pai kumhiar* (*Var Asa Mehalla I Ādigranth* p. 466). The word *beiman* is said to have been substituted for the word *musalman* by Ram Rai, and thus, he won over the Emperor.

54. Trilochan Singh *op. cit.* p. 121.

55. Ibid. See : Chapter XI "Guru Baba Found" pp. 120--148

56-57. *Ibid.* p. 313

58. *Ibid.* p. 299

59. His Four companions were i. Bhai Mati Das ii. Bhai Sati Das, iii. Bhai Dayal Das and iv. Bhai Gurdita. First three were beheaded by the orders of Emperor Aurangzeb.

60. See Chapter 5.

61. Only Ratan Singh Bhangu holds the view that the Guru created *Khālsā* in 1695. See *Panth Prakash* pp. 43-44.

62. Santokh Singh "Importance of Amrit" pp. 22-23.

63. Khushwant Singh, *op. cit.* p. 84; Hari Ram Gupta *History of the Sikh Gurus* p. 159 Macauliffe, *op. cit.* vol. v. pp. 23, 95, Malcolm, *The Sikhs* p. 221.

64-65. Khushwant Singh, *op. cit.* p. 89.

66-67. Jagjit Singh, *The Sikh Revolution* p, 145.

68. Ganda Singh, "Raj karega Khālsā couplet" in The *Singh Sabha and other Socio-Religious Movement in the Panjab*, p. 199.

69. Ibid, p. 201.

70 "Bacitar Natak" in Dasam Granth p, 57.

71. Kishan Singh, *op. cit.*, p. 114.

CHAPTER 3

THE SIKH-STATE RELATIONS

The trilogy is conceived in the background of turbulent period of about thirty five years in the history of the Panjab, spread over between 1726 and 1761. This period, when viewed in a wider perspective, forms a small fragment of an historical epoch invariably referred to by historians characterising decline of the Mughal Empire. A number of causes are enumerated that accelerated the decline of the Mughal Empire, but "the two most important were the rise of the Maraṭhas and the Sikhs."[1] Our main concern, at present, is to ascertain the relations between the Sikhs and the State during the period under review.

Kirpal Singh,[2] an eminent Sikh historian, has worked out the details of the period from 1726-1761, described in the trilogy. *Sundri* depicts the span of about twentysix years from 1726-1752. In 1726 Zakariya Khan (r. 1726-1745) became the governor of Lahore and was succeeded by his son Yahya Khan (r. 1745-1748) in 1745. *Sundri* concludes its journey with the death of Dewan Kauṛa Mal that occured in 1752 during the regime of Mir Mannu (r. 1748-1753) who became the governor of the Panjab in 1748. Mir Mannu died in 1753 and after his death his widow Begam Mughlani from 1753 to 1757 was, in actual practice, at the helm of the State of the Panjab. *Bijay Singh* covers the period from 1751-1752 and thus concludes with the fourth invasion of Ahmad Shah Abdali in 1756-1757. *Satwant Kaur* starts with the rule of

Timur Shah (son of Abdali) in the Panjab and describing the disorderly phase from 1756-1757 onward comes to an end describing some events of the year 1761.

For most of the time, during this period the State of the Panjab was under the jurisdiction of the Mughal Emperors at the Centre.

Muhammad Mu'azzam, the eldest son of Emperor Aurangzeb after the death of his father, successfully eliminating his younger brothers, A'zam and Kambaksh, ascended the throne of the Mughal Empire, under the title of Bahadur Shah, at the age of sixty-four in 1707 and died in the year 1712. The war of succession, now, began among the sons of Bahadur Shah. Jahandar Shah came out victorious and captured the throne of Delhi. He remained Emperor just for one year during 1712-1713 and was deposed and murdered by Farrukhsiyar the grandson of Bahadur Shah, at Agra in 1713. Farrukhsiyar became the new Emperor by the support of Sayyid Brothers—Abdu'llah Khan and Husain Ali Khan Barha also known as 'kingmakers'—he was, in a way, under obligation to allow the sovereignty to pass into the hands of Sayyid Brothers. He was an Emperor in name only. He made attempts to rid himself of the supremacy of the Sayyid Brothers and was strangled instead in 1719. Sayyid Brothers installed weak phantom kings such as Rafiud-darajat, Rafiud-dault (Shahjahan II), Nekusiyar and Ibrahim and finally Muhammad Shah who got Husain killed and Abdullah imprisoned. Muhammad Shah (r. 1719-1748) was hardly eighteen when he occupied the throne as Mughal Emperor in 1719 and was succeeded by his eldest son Ahmad Shah in 1748, the year he died. Ahmad Shah was blinded by his *wazir* Ghazi-ud-din in 1754 and as a result of that son of Jahandar Shah under the title of Alamgir II ascended the throne of Delhi. Ali Gawhar, the son of Alamgir II killed his father in 1759 at the instance of the Emperor's prime minister, and the throne of Delhi passed on to the son who assumed the title of Shah Alam II, yet another phantom Emperor, as, in fact, Delhi was practically under the control of the Marathas. In the year 1761 Ahmad Shah Abdali defeated Marathas in the Third Battle of Panipat. "The Mughal Empire", in the words of Bipin Chandra," had by 1761 ceased to exist in practice as an all-India Empire", and "it remained merely as the Kingdom of Delhi."[3]

A passing reference has been made hitherto to the Rulers at the Centre and in the State of the Panjab in order to touch upon the political milieu and, thus, gradually, to arrive at the centre of our problem. The policy of the State was, by and large, to oppress the Sikhs and who in turn refused to be cowed down by the oppressive measures adoped by the Rulers. The State machinery was let loose, time and again, to persecute the Sikhs. The sad story of mass persecution of the Sikhs at the hands of the Rulers of the Panjab in league with the Rulers at the Centre, that followed during our period, begins with the execution of Banda Bahadur. The Mughal Emperor Furrukhsiyar (r. 1713-1719) ordered a punitive expedition against Banda Bahadur under the command of the Delhi *wazir* Qamarud-Din Khan, assisted by Zain-ud-Din Khan, the governor of Sirhand, and Abd-us-Samad Khan, the governor of the Panjab and his son Zakariya Khan, the governor of Jammu, to arrest and produce Banda Bahadur alive in the royal court, in Delhi. After hunting down Banda Bahadur the royal troops captured him alive alongwith his followers in December 1715 from the *haveli* of Dunichand at village Gurdas Nangal in Gurdaspur. The execution of Banda Bahadur and his surviving followers started in the year 1716, in Delhi. Over 700 Sikhs were beheaded near Kotwali in Chandni Chowk, Delhi, when each one of them refused to accept the offer of abandoning their religious faith in favour of the Faith of the Emperor. The same offer was made to Banda Bahadur who, obviously, had declined the offer and was executed on June 9, 1716 in the vicinity of Qutab Minar, in Delhi.[4]

"The execution of the Sikh leader, Banda Bahadur"[5] and "the elimination of the Sikh power from the Panjab"[6] is hailed by S. A. A Rizvi as "the most striking achievement of Farrukhsiyar."[7] Rizvi is not wrong, at least, in pointing out the facts of the history as regard to the elimination of the Sikh power from the Panjab The State machinery did not stop there, rather, accelerated the process, now, that of eliminating the Sikhs. "The Emperor [Farrukhsiyar] then issued a general edict, "which was applicable to all parts of the Empire."[8] As regard to the measures to be taken, as advised in the said edict, for the annihilation of the Sikhs, in the words of Hari Ram Gupta were :

> According to it every Sikh wherever seen was to be immediately arrested. He was to be offered only one alternative, either Islam or sword. It was to be executed there and then without any hesitation or loss of time. A schedule of valuable rewards was proclaimed. For every Sikh head Rs. 25 was to be given, and for a Sikh captive a sum of Rs. 100 was to be awarded. Their pretty girls were to be reduced to concubines, and others to be made maid servants. When a Muslim died his grave was to be dug by the Sikhs or their Hindu sympathisers. For *begar* (unpaid labour), in place of cobblers Sikhs were to be employed."[9]

Abd-us-Samad Khan, the governor of the Panjab was deputed to get the edict implemented in letter and spirit. Now, there were only two options open for the Sikhs : either to become clean-shaven or be determined to remain the *Khālsā*. The *Khālsā* fled to *Shivalik* hills and *Lakhi Jungle*. Bhai Vir Singh has described these thick forests in the second chapter of *Sundri*. The forest on account of consisting of hundred thousand trees is known as *Lakhi Jungle*. It is this *Lakhi Jungle* that the Sikhs had made their home, alright, but the problem was how to survive. "For them [*the Khālsā*]" writes Khushwant Singh "the only way of survival was the way of out laws—to plunder State treasuries and the homes of the rich."[10] The homeless *Khālsā* were terror but not for the poor and the innocent people. Not only that the *Khālsā* had left their homes, they were left with no leaders, as well. The institution of *Gurmatā* that came into existence during the times of Guru Gobind Singh, was now revived through convening the *Sarbat-Khālsā* . The *Sarbat Khālsā*, in those days, was a biennial affair when the Sikhs used to assemble at Amritsar on the day of *Baisākhī* and at *Dīwalī* festival. The problems that the Sikh community was facing were discussed at length. After the deliberations made to the fullest satisfaction of those present, the resolutions were passed and termed as *Gurmatā*. The *Sarbat Khālsā* and its outcome *Gurmatā* were truly democratic in nature aiming at to serve the interests of the community as against the interests of the person/persons. In pursuance of the *Gurmatā* the *Jathedāras* were appointed and delegated powers to arrive at peaceful settlement with the concerned authorities.[11]

Zakariya Khan the son of Abd-us-Samad Khan, with the connivance of Nawab Qamar-ud-Din Khan, who was former's brother in law (from wife) and the prime minister of Muhammad Shah, the Mughal Emperor, became the governor of

Lahore in 1726 and after the death of his father in 1737, Multun, earlier, forming a part of the Panjab also came under his jurisdiction. Zakariya Khan had deployed *Gaśti Fauj*[12] throughout the province and the only duty assigned to it was to arrest the Sikhs and send them to Lahore. Giving informations about the where-about of the Sikhs was a flourishing business. Despite these measures the Sikhs upheld the dignity of their community. Describing the state of mind of the Sikhs during this period of hardships, Hari Ram Gupta writes :

> These men remained as brave as a lion, as fearless as a tiger and as firm as rock. No pain, no hardship, no affliction, no mortification, no vexation, no agony, and no suffering could shake off their determination and could make them falter or flicker from their objective."[13]

The Sikhs did not lose their balance and poise. "Residence in wilderness" adds Hari Ram Gupts, "made them fiery and ferocious like tigers, bears and cobras only for their foes, while they remained gentle, mild, sober, soft, cool and quite for their friends and sympathisers. Love of liberty never allowed them to bend their heads."[14]

Zakariya Khan like his father Abd-us-Samad Khan realized his utter failure to suppress the Sikhs. He changed his policy from suppression to pacification of the Sikhs and wore a mask of benign policy towards them.

In 1733 Zakariya Khan, after toiling at the idea of eliminating the Sikhs, again, during seven years of his rule as governor of Lahore, at last adopted a conciliatory approach to the problems posed by he Sikhs and sent some envoy to meet them making an offer of a *jāgīr*, comprising the area of Dipalpur, Kanganwal and Jhabal and a title of *Nawāb*.[15] The said offer was accepted and Kapur Singh (d. 1753) was made the *Nawāb*. Now, the *Khālsā* abandoned their hideouts and for a while were no more out laws. The *Khālsā* settled at Amritsar in the vicinity of *Harimandir Sahib* (The Golden Temple). Then, there arose a quarrel between the younger and the old people constituting the fraternity of the *Khālsā* over the distribution of the supplies. The *Khālsā* were divided into the *Taruṇa Dal* (the younger) and the *Buḍhā Dal* (the elder), to facilitate the smooth working within. But, later on both the *Dals* (groups) got divided into number of small groups headed by their group-leaders.[16] A section of *Taruṇa Dal* after reviewing the overall political situation and their general plight resolved that nothing but freedom from oppression was their goal and 'adjustments' were no solutions to their problems. So this section of the *Khālsā* revolted against the State and started collecting revenue besides adopting such other measures derecognizing the authority of the State. Zakariya Khan offered recruitment to the 'frustrated lot' in the army, but the *Khālsā* declined to accept the offer and by way of retaliation Zakariya Khan confiscated the *jāgīr*, allotted to the *Khālsā*, as a gesture of goodwill.[17] The *Khālsā*, once again took to 'wandering in the wilderness.'

It was during the reign of Zakariya Khan that Bhai Mani Singh the head-priest of *Harimandir Sahib* was tortured to death in the year 1738.[18] Bhai Mani Singh had asked the permission to celebrate *Diwālī* at Amritsar in 1738 and it was granted against the payment of Rs. 5,000 to the State authorities after the celebrations were over. This huge amount, naturally, was to be paid out of the collection made as a result of offering by the Sikhs. Zakariya Khan deployed huge force as if he was concerned about the law and order in the city and in the welfare of the Sikhs. The Sikhs got scared of the Mughal army and did not turn up in large number, with the result that the expected sum of money could not be collected. Bhai Mani Singh, on account of non-payment of dues, was arrested and taken to Lahore. He was offered clemency, in case, he would embrace Islam. Bhai Mani Singh, had no choice other than embracing death. The execution of Bhai Mani Singh inflicted another injury to the Sikh-psyche.

The same year Nadir Shah, the king of Persia, invaded India. The brutalities of the invader's army forced the inhabitants of the province of the Panjab to leave their homes and to take refuge in the hills. Zakariya Khan the then governor of the province of the Panjab having failed to stand up against the Persian army surrendered. The surrender of Zakariya Khan, of course, helped Nadir Shah to advance to Delhi, but the Mughal army marched from Delhi to resist and confronted Nadir Shah at Karnal on 13th February 1739. The Mughal army was defeated and Muhammad Shah, the Mughal Emperor, was taken prisoner. Nadir Shah entered Delhi in early March 1739 and captured the royal treasury and looted the richmen of Delhi. He had also ordered a general massacre of the citizens of Delhi to avenge the killing of a few of his soldiers.

After staying for about five months (from the end of December 1738 to the end of May, 1739) "Nadir Shah returned to Persia ...having bestowed the Empire of Hindustan on Muhammad Shah as his own free gift."[19] And under the treaty Muhammad Shah ceded the provinces of Sind and Kabul and four districts of the province of Lahore forming a part of the Mughal Empire. While going back to Persia the Sikhs seized a large quantity of booty from Nadir Shah.[20]

Nadir Shah's departure is marked by Zakariya Khan's attempt to restore law and order in the province- Zakariya Khan arrived at the conclusion that since the Sikhs were inimical to 'peace and progress' they should be forced to obedience. To subdue the Sikhs Zakariya Khan resolved to take stern measures against them and as follow up action issued instructions to the roving columns to attack the fort at Dallewal situated on the banks of the rive *Ravi*. The fort was completely demolished. the large number of Sikhs were killed then and there and about ten thousand thus arrested were taken to Lahore in chains and publicly executed at the place known as *Shahid Ganj*, place of martyrdom, in the Sikh history[21] Zakariya Khan had deputed Adina Beg to drive away the Sikhs from Jullundur *Doab* as the latter had moved to this part of the province. But the Sikhs continued their struggle, as usual. The governerment too was determined to wipe out the Sikhs, therefore, according to General John J. H. Gordon :

> A proclamation was issued by the Lahore Viceroy [Zakariya Khan] ordering a general massacre of the long-haired Singhs wherever found. They were hunted like wild beasts, a price being placed on their heads; thousands were put to death, refusing pardon on the condition of renouncing their faith and cutting their hair.[22]

As a result of sustained efforts of the government to eliminate the entire Sikh community the Sikhs were forced to leave the Panjab and to make hills of Jammu and Kangra, deserts of Bikaner and Malwa and the forests of *Lakhi Jungle* as their homes. During the period of exile the Sikhs did not deviate from the path and "they," [the Sikhs] while categorising the Sikhs, Hari Ram Gupta states "came from that class which in times of disaster is always privileged to suffer. But while they groaned they meditated, while they dreamt they hoped, while they suffered, they aspired."[23] Again, "as their hardships grew greater, the more frequent became their prayers (*ardās*)."[24]

A number of the Sikhs, besides Bhai Mani Singh, were tortured to death during the reign of Zakariya Khan. One such martyr was Bhai Taru Singh.[25] He was hardly in early twenties and his only sin was that he used to send food to the Sikhs taking shelter in forests. Bhai Taru Singh was arrested and asked to make a choice between Islam and death. He preferred death and was tortured on the wheel and later on died and was cremated on 25th June 1743 in *Shahid Ganj* at Lahore.

During the period under review to hurt and humiliate the Sikhs, *Harimandir Sahib* at Amritsar, the holy place of the Sikhs, was made an object of several sacrilegious attacks. Amritsar the city, earlier known as Ram Das Pur or *Guru Ka Cakk* was founded by Guru Ram Das the fourth Guru of the Sikhs. The Golden Temple consists of holy tank and *Harimandir Sahib* constructed in the midst of the tank or *sarovar*. The construction of the holy tank, under the supervision of Guru Arjan Dev the fifth Guru of the Sikhs was completed in 1589. The construction of holy tank was started by Bhai Jeṭha (later on Guru Ram Das) in 1573 at the command of Guru Amar Das the third Guru of the Sikhs. Guru Arjan Dev got it only completed, but the idea to build *Harīmandir Sahib* was his own. Mian Mir, a *Sūfi* saint, who hailed from Sistan in Central Asia, now the resident of Lahore at the request of Guru Arjan Dev, laid the foundation stone of *Harimandir Sahib* which was completed in the year 1601. Guru Har Gobind the sixth Guru, built *Akāl Takhat* (also called *Akāl Buṅgā*) in 1609 to further add into the glory and significance of *Harimandir Sahib*. The sixth Guru also wore two swords, referred to as of *Mirī* and *Pīrī*. One sword of *Mirī* (short form of *amīrī* i. e. richness) signified temporal power, whereas the sword of

Pīrī (saintliness) symbolized spiritual power. Spiritual and temporal were conceived forming an integrated whole.

In the history of sacrilegious attacks[26] made on *Harimandir Sahib* the name of Massa Ranghar continues to prick in the Sikh psyche. Zakariya Khan made Massa Ranghar the resident of village Mandiala, in Amritsar, the incharge of *Harimandir Sahib* with instructions to 'teach a lesson' to the Sikhs. Massa Ranghar occupied *Harimandir Sahib* and to demoralize and psychologically destroy the Sikhs, converted it into a 'Place of Pleasure'. Thus, he undermined the sanctity of the holy place of the Sikhs. This was not to be tolerated at any cost, any longer. So, to avenge wrong done by Massa Ranghar, Sukha Singh and Mehtab Singh beheaded him right in the four walls of *Harimandir Sahib* when he was drunk and indulging in the company of dancing girls.

Zakariya Khan's attempts to annihilate the Sikhs came to an end with his death in July, 1745.

Yahya Khan succeeded his father Zakariya Khan as a governor of Lahore. This change of person while continuing with the old policy of the Rulers wanting extinction of the Sikh community, rather made the Sikhs more apprehensive. In such a situation any community for its survival must prepare itself to confront the hostile forces. The Sikhs, by now, who were scattered forming small *jathās* (groups), in order to survive the crisis the community was faced with, assembled on the *Dīwālī* festival of 1745 at Amritsar and converting the assembly of the Sikhs into *Sarbat Khālsā* resolved to reorgnise themselves into twentyfive Sikh regiments under the Supreme Command of Nawab Kapur Singh. After rallying under one Supreme Commander the Sikhs dissuaded the farmers from paying revenue to the State, eliminated number of *Caudharies* and *muqaddams*, who operated as informers against them and destroyed quite a few towns.[27] Thereafter the Sikhs plundered Lahore. The State authorities under the orders of Yahya Khan came forward to dispel the rebels and during this brawl that took place sometimes in March 1746, Jaspat Rai, the *faujdār* of Eminabad and who was the brother of Diwan Lakhpat Rai, was killed. Jaspat Rai was instrumental in getting Bhai Mani Singh arrested and all the more reason that the Sikhs were itching to settle scores with him. Ratan Singh Bhangu[28] and Giani Gian Singh,[29] both the Sikh chroniclers have recorded almost indentical outbursts of Diwan Lakhpat Rai on the occasion of killing of his brother by Sikh soldiers. Lakhpat Rai, as stated in the Sikh chronicles expressed his anger before Yahya Khan, hurling his turban on the floor—

Sworn that he would go bareheaded until he had destroyed the Sikhs.[30]

And, further reiterated that :

> I am a *Kshatriya* but I shall not call myself by that name until I have erased their [*Khālsā*] name from the page of existence.[31]

In pursuance of his vow Lakhpat Rai, with Mughal army under his command, chased the *Khālsā*, and by the Mughal army, according to the estimate of Ratan Singh Bhangu,[32] about seven thousand *Khālsā* were butchered and three thousand were taken as prisoners, later on, tortured to death at *Sahid Ganj* in Lahore during the moth of June 1746. This mass persecution of the Sikhs goes into the annals of the Sikh history under the name of *Choṭā ghalūghārā* (the minor bloody carnage).[33]

When after the death of Zakariya Khan in 1745, his son Yahya Khan managed to become the governor of Lahore, Shah Nawaz the younger brother of Yahya Khan had accepted to be the governor of Multan. But this compromise between the brothers did not last long. Shah Nawaz took to arms against Yahya Khan and in the month of March 1747 attacked Lahore, captured the city, arrested his brother and put him into prison. Now, Shah Nawaz after annexing the province of Lahore, was the governor of the Panjab. He also put Lakhpat Rai into jail. Shah Nawaz chose Kauṛa Mal as his *Dīwān* and took Adina Beg (formerly the governor of Jallandur during the reign of Zakariya Khan), in to confidence. Yahya Khan somehow managed to break loose from the prison and thus Shah Nawaz was in a dwindling position when on the advice of Adina Beg he allured Ahmad Shah Abdali to make an inroad to India.

Chaos and confusion always helps the Rebels. The Sikhs made full use of such a state of affairs to regain their strength and as an evidence to that they built a fortress, *Ram Rauni* as resolved in the *Sarbat Khālsā* convened on the day of *Baisākhi* in the year 1747.

Ahmad Shah Abdali, the Afgan king, at the instance of Shah Nawaz, forced his way to Labore and arrived there in January 1748. He plundered the city, stayed in Lahore for about a month and proceeded to Delhi, the capital of Mughal Empire.

The Mughal army under the Command of *Wazir* Qamarudin resisted the Afghan troops in the way, near Sirhand. In the event of Wazir's death in this battle, his son Muiṅ-ul-Mulk forced the Afghans to withdraw from their positions. Again, there was a chaos in the political set-up. The *Khāisā* under the leadership of Jassa Singh Ahluwalia by defeating Adina Beg at Hoshiarpur improved their image as a force to reckon with. To keep up their image the *Khālsā* on the advice of Jassa Singh Ahluwalia, the Commander of one of the Sikh regiment, decided in the *Sarbat Khālsa* held on the day of *Baisākhi* in the year 1748, to dissolve twentyfive regiments and eonstitute the *Dal Khālsā*. The *Dal Khālsa* was a name given to the Sikh army put under the Command of Jassa Singh Ahluwalia, who, further divided it into eleven big *Jathās* later on known as *misals*, enjoying equal status.

Muin-ul-Mulk, generally referred to as Mir Mannu in Sikh history, had successfully fought against the Afghans, keeping this fact in view the Mughal Emperor Muhammad Shah appointed him as the governor of the Panjab. Soon after his appointment in April 1748, Mir Mannu resolved to establish law and order in the State of the Panjab. Mir Mannu was hostile to the Sikhs and there were forces hostile to Mir Mannu, also. One such force was Safdar Jang, the *Wazir* at Delhi, whose survival depended upon the destruction of Mir Mannu, the latter being the leader of Turks. The battle for power was being fought at the level of clan-conflict.

It has been the part of the Sikh tradition to celebrate *Baisākhi* and *Dīwālī* at *Harimandir Sahib* come what may. The Sikhs from all parts of the province arrived at Amritsar in October 1749 to celcbrate *Dīwālī* at *Harimandir Sahib*. The Rulers, at times, had shown a gesture of goodwill and friendliness towards the Sikhs, but the latter were never sure about the conduct of the Rulers. The Sikhs, therefore were vigilant to safeguard their interests. When the Sikhs assembled to celebrate *Dīwālī*, about five hundred stayed at *Ram Rauṇi* fort as a measure to fight back, if the need be. The fears of the Sikhs were not illusionary. Mir Mannu thought it to be a golden opportunity to crush the Sikhs, and assisted by Adina Beg besieged the fort that continued for four months and after about two hundred Sikhs were killed the siege was raised at the intervention of Diwan Kauṛa Mal. This settlement between the Rulers and the Sikhs was not going to last long as the Sikhs realized that the 'adjustments' with the Rulers—the kind of the Rules they had—were certainly contrary to the Sikh Ideal.

Ahmad Shah Abdali invaded India second time during the reign of Mir Mannu in December 1749. Mir Mannu asked for the help from the Centre which was refused. The Mughal Emperor Ahmad Shah instead agreed to part with revenue of the *Cahar mahal* comprising Auraugabad (in Jhelum) Gujrat Sialkot and Pasrur as demanded by Ahmad Shah Abdali in his letter addressed to Mir Mannu.

When Mir Mannu was involved in fighting against the Afghan troops on the banks of river *Cenāb* and his deputy had left Lahore to resist the advance of Jahan Khan, the General of Afghan army, the Sikhs finding it 'smooth sailing' plundered Lahore and this act of the Sikhs naturally enraged Mir Mannu, who ordered the killing of the Sikhs wherever, found.[34]

Ahmad Shah Abdali after invading India second time and making arrangements for procuring revenue of the *Cahār mahal* returned. He again, i.e. third time, in December 1751 forced his way to India, since the revenue due to him was not paid. Abdali sent a messenger to Mir Mannu in the respect of non-payment of revenue,[35] not satisfied with the explanations put forth by Mir Mannu such as, dīsturbances in the province etc. marched towards Lahore beseiged the city which lasted for four months. It was during this period (December 1751 to March 1752) that Diwan Kauṛa Mal was shot dead. Mir Mannu, at least, surrendered and the treaty was signed through which the provinces of Lahore and Multan passed on to Abdali and it was, later on, countersigned by the Emperor Ahmad Shah. Under the said treaty Panjab ceded to Afghan Empire.

Whenever Mir Mannu found respite he took up his arms against the Sikhs and got thousands of Sikhs killed. "Once on the day of Īd" writes Maulvi Nur Ahmad Chiśti, "he [Mir Mannu] beheaded 1100 Sikhs."[36] The atrocities of Mir Mannu committed against the Sikhs have become part of the Sikh-psyche and the same are preserved in Panjabi jingling verse that reads :

> Mir Mannu is our Sickle
> We the fodder for him to mow,
> The more he reaps, the more we grow.[37]

Mir Mannu died of poisoning by one of his officers in November 1753 and after his death his widow Begam Mughlani took over the charge of the affairs of the Panjab. After his death the Sikhs took revenge.[38] In fact, the Mughal Emperor Amhad Shah had appointed the three years old son of Mir Mannu named Mahmud Khan as a governor of the Panjab and his two years old son Muhammad Amin as a deputy. Whereas, technically the province of the Panjab was to be administered by Mumin Khan, the Deputy of Abdali, but in actual practice Begam Mughlani was the Sovereign of the Panjab. Abdali, under whose jurisdiction the province of the Panjab has been since 1752 also agreed to the arrangements proposed as his main objective was to secure revenue.

When Muhammad Amin Khan died in May 1754 Begam Mughlani on her own assumed the reins of the government of the Panjab simultaneously seeking approval from both the Ahmad Shahs.[39] Later on, when Alamgir II the Mughal Emperor favoured Mumin Khan in appointing him as the governor in 1754, Begam Mughlani rendered him ineffective, Contemporary chroniclers are in agreement in the respect of Begam being of liscentious nature.[40] This liscentiousness of the Ruler led the State of the Panjab into disintegration.

Already, Multan and the districts of Gujrat, Sialkot, Aurangabad, and Pasrur were under the sovereign control of the Afghan king, Abdali. A good number of principalities had come into existence further adding into the amorphous nature of political set-up of the province of the Panjab. Besides that the Panjab had nine governors within the short span of three years from November 1753 to October, 1756.[41] In the absence of any worthy Ruler the Sikhs, who were a strong force, took upon themselves the obligations of the Ruler. The Sikh Rulers or the *misals* provided *rākhi* or protection to the people of the Panjab against some compensation for their services rendered to them.

Begam Mughlani although a shrewed woman aided by her liscentious nature could not eclipse her adversaries for a long time and was arrested in March 1756. While in prison at Delhi she sent a word to Ahmad Shah Abdali telling him that, "If you invade India this time, the Indian Empire with all its riches will fall into your hands."[42] Abdali, prompted by temptation for wamen and greed for wealth, made an inroad to India for the fourth time, crossing Lahore, he reached Delhi in January 1757. He sacked the city of Delhi and with the promised assistance of Begam Mughlani, looted the noble's families and captured host of female slaves and concubines. He also extended his territory by annexing Sirhand and adding it into the province of the Panjab.

The Afghans, carrying off immense booty, left Delhi in April 1757 for their homeward journey. On the way back, the Sikhs under the Command of Sardar Ala Singh robbed Prince Taimur of his booty at Sanawar and Malerkoṭla. Abdali adopted suitable measures to guard against the attacks made by the Sikhs but of no avail. He was quite desperate as he could not successfully meet the onslaught of the Sikhs. On arriving at Lahore, to avenge his humilation suffered at the hands of the Sikhs, he ordered the blowing up of *Harimāndir Sahib* and to add insult to injury Abdali got the holy tank polluted by dumping with slaughtered cows.

Abdali left for home leaving behind Prince Taimur as a Sovereign of the Panjab.[43] The Sikhs were feeling restless on account of Abdali's sacrilegious attacks on *Harimandir Sahib.* There was no escape, therefore, from a clash between the Sikhs and the Afghan troops. Baba Deep Singh, head of a *misal,* expressed his desire that he was under an obligation to rebuild *Harimandir Sanib* as it was placed under his care and control. He marched towards Amritsar leading an army of about five thousand Sikhs, joining him gradually on the way, armed with deadly weapons. Jahan Khan, the General of Afghan army, in order to frustrate the plan of Baba Deep Singh, alongwith large force, also moved towards Amritsar. In the battle, Baba Deep Singh received fatal injuties. The Afghan troops, once again, violated the sacredness of *Harimandir Sahib.*

The Sikhs were not to sleep over the descreation of their holy shrine. Jassa Singh Ahluwalia inspired the Sikhs to take revengc of the sacrilegious attack on *Harimandir Sahib.* The Sikh army while fighting against the Afghans at Mahipalpur, in District Hoshiarpur miserably defeated them. Despite the fact that Tamur despatched huge army to crush the Sikhs, the Afghan army was not only defeated, but was also relieved of guns and ammunitions. It was really humiliating for the Ruler.

Adina Beg Khan true to his Machiavellian nature not only persuaded the Marat̤has to invade the Panjab but also manoeuvred full support of the Sikhs for the Marat̤has pitted against the Afghans.[44] As planned, the Marat̤hā army under the Command of Raghu Nath Rao, made an inroad to the Panjab in March 1758 and in this operation the Sikhs rendered full help in securing Sirhand. The Afghan army could not resist the joint front of the Sikh and the Maraṭha armies and as a result of the failure on their part were forced to give up their control over the city of Lahore.

When both the Sikh and the Maraṭha armies captured Lahore in April 1758, they searched for the Prince Tamur and General Jahan Khan. Both of them finally escaped. In order to provide some relief to their injured psyche the Sikhs brought Afghan soldiers to Amritsar and forced them to clean up the *Sarovar* (Holy tank) they had polluted.

The Maraṭhas, after their successful expedition against the Afghans had returned to Delhi. Again in March, 1759, the Maraṭhas forced their way to the Panjab as a matter of political strategy to capture Lahore. The Maraṭhas with the help of the Sikh army, once again forced the Afghan army to retire.

For the fifth time in autumn of 1759 Ahmad Shah Abdali with huge force invaded India at the request of Muslim rulers settled throughout the country to protect Islam from militant Hinduism.[45] The Sikhs faced the Afghan troops when they arrived in Lahore and killed about two thousand of them whereas, Sabaji who was the General of Maratha army abruptly left the Panjab. Then the Sikhs did hot check the Afghan troops on the way and they marched without any resistance towards Delhi.

Bhai Vir Singh in the last chapter (17th) of *Satwant Kaur* has referred to Abdali's march to Delhi but his description is confined to killing of nobles at Delhi; his crushing defeat to Marathas of Mathura and plundering of temples and the city and his return to Delhi, where he stayed for three months and robbed the rich men of their wealth.

And, on his way back to his home land, Abdali in March 1761 appointed Zain Khan as the governor of Sirhand.[46]

The Sikhs fought against the oppression of the Rulers at home and Nadir Shah and Abdali the aggressors. The Rulers and the aggressors, both were concerned to rule over and exploit the people irrespective of their religious affinity and to fulfil their ambitions never hesitated to fight against the people belonging to their own Faith.

In fact, it was Ruler the villain the Sikhs fought against.

References and Notes

1. Khushwant Singh. *A History of the Sikhs* Vol. I. p. 120.
2. Kirpal Singh, "Historical Significance of *Sundri, Bijay Singh* and *Satwant Kaur*" in Ganda Singh (Ed) *Bhai Vir Singh* (Birth Centenary Volume) pp. 84, 86.
3. Bipin Chandra, *Modern India* p. 8.
4. For details regarding the ugly manner in which Banda was brought in procession to Delhi, see : W. L. M'Gregor, *The History of the Sikhs* Vol. I pp. 109-110. An execution of Banda Bahadur is also referred to in *Satwant Kaur* p. 97.

   And the way the son of Banda Bahadur was killed and his limbs were thrust in the mouth of Banda Bahadur, for detailed description, see : Khafi Khan, *Munata khab-Ul-Lubab* Vol. II pp. 766-767.
   Also see : Elphinstone, *History of India* p. 686.

   Regarding the controversy over the place of execution see : Ganda Singh, "The place of Baba Banda Singh's Execution" in *Journal of Sikh Studies* Vol. II, No. 2 August, 1975 pp. 117-131.

5-7. S A.A. Rizvi, *The Wonder That was India* Vol. II p. 149.

8-9. Hari Ram Gupta, *History of the Sikhs* vol. II p. 39.

10. Khushwant Singh *op. cit.* p. 121.

11. For details, see : Bhagat Singh, "The Institution of *Gurmatā*" in *Journal of Sikh Studies* vol. IV No. 2. August, 1977 pp. 99-108.

    Bhai Vir Singh has also referred to passing of various *Gurmatās* in *Sundri* and *Satwant Kaur*. *Sundri* : pp 79, 80, 82; *Satwant Kaur* : pp. 131, 139, 199-200, 206-207, 231-232, 241-244, 246-247, 249, 251, 292, 302.

12. Bhai Vir Singh has referred to *Gaśtī Fauj* in *Sundri* p. 72.

13-14. Hari Ram Gupta *op. cit.* pp. 45-46.

15. However, there is a controversy as regard to the name of envoy and the place where the offer was made and accepted. see :

    i. Teja Singh and Ganda Singh, *A Short History of Sikhs* pp. 121, 129-130.

    ii. Ratan Singh Bhangu *Pracīn Panth Prakaś* pp. 210-217.

    iii. Gian Singh, *Panth Prakaś* pp. 649-650 :

    iv. Hari Ram Gupta, *op. cit.* pp. 46-47.

    v. Khushwant Singh, *op. cit.* pp- 122-123.

    Also referred to in *Satwant Kaur* pp. 199-200.

16. Gian Singh, *op. cit.* pp. 500 ff.

17. *Satwant Kaur* p. 200.

18. Gurtej Singh, "*Bhai Mani Singh in Historical Prospective*" in *Proceedings of the Panjab History Conference* Patiala 1968, pp. 120-127.

    Reference to an execution of Bhai Mani Singh is made in the dialogue between Bijay Singh and his mother in *Bijay Singh* p. 9.

19. James Brown, Major, "History of the Origin and Progress of the Sicks (Sikhs)" in Ganda Singh (Ed.) *Early European Accounts of the Sikhs* p. 131.

20. George Forester, *A Journey From Bengal to England* vol. I. p. 313; *Satwant Kaur* p. 178.

21. Nur Ahmad Chiśti *Tahqiqat-e-Chiśti* p. 101.

22. John. J.H. Gordon, *History of the Sikhs* p. 50.

23-24. Hari Ram Gupta, *op. cit.* pp. 61, 62.

25. *Bijay Singh*, pp. 13, 186.

26. Gian Singh, *op. cit.* pp. 711ff.

Reference to Massa Ranghar in *Sundri* p. 72.

27. *Ibid* pp. 771-772.

28. Ratan Singh Bhangu, *op. cit.* pp. 291-293.

Killing of Jaspat Rai by the Sikhs is referred to in *Sundri* p. 56.

29. Gian Singh, *op. cit.* pp. 775-776.

Reference to Jaspat Rai in getting Bhai Mani Singh arrested in *Sundri* p. 60.

30-31. Khushwant Singh *op. cit.* p. 129 n.
Also see : *Sundri* p. 56.

32. Ratan Singh Bhangu. *op. cit.* p. 296.

Bhai Vir Singh has referred to atrocities committed by Lakhpat Rai against the Sikhs in *Sundri* at pp. 32, 54-62, 65, 71 and Chapter 13 of *Sundri* (*Choṭā Ghalū Ghārā*).

33. Ganda Singh, *History of the Gurdwara of Shahid Ganj Lahore*, pp. 30-31.

Bhai Vir Singh has also described it in Chapter 13 of *Sundri*.

34. Khushwaqt Rai, *Twarikh-i-Sikkhān* or *Kitab-i-Twarikh-i-Panjab* p. 73.

35. *Satwant Kaur* p. 205 n.

36. Nur Ahmad Chisti, *op. cit.* pp. 82 ff.
Regarding the persecution of the Sikhs during the rule of Mir Mannu see :
P. Setu Mahdva Rao (Abd. Trs) *Tahmas Namā* p. 19.

37. i. Nur Ahmad Chisti. *op. cit.* p. 100 :

Mir Mannu Sāḍhi dātrī
Asin Mir Mannu de soe
Jiyon Jiyon Sahnū wadhdā
Asin sau sau dūṇe hoe

ii. Khuswant Singh, *op. cit.* p. 140.

Bhai Vir Singh also quoted it in *Satwant Kaur* p. 197.

38. *Bijay Singh* pp. 114.

39. *Idem.*

40. Tahmas Khan Miskin, *Tazkira-i-Tahmas* (1780) pp. 99, 122, 159-160, 230-231. Quoted in Hari Ram Gupta *op. cit.* p. 287 n.
Also see : P. Setu Mahdav Rao *op. cit.* p. 101.
Bhai Vir Singh has devoted 15th, 17th, 18th, 19th, 20th and 22nd chapters of *Bijay Singh* to describe the life and character of Begam Mughlani and has clearly depicted her licentiousness and advances she made towards Bijay Singh, when in her captivity.

41. Hari Ram Gupta *op. cit.* pp. 123-124 n.

42. Aliuddin, *Ībarat Nama* p. 114. Quoted in Khushwant Singh *op. cit.* p, 143.
Also referred to in *Satwant Kaur* pp. 128-130.

43. It was during this fourth invasion of Abdali when Satwant Kaur was taken as a captive to Kabul. See : *Satwant Kaur* pp. 130, 132.

44. *Satwant Kaur* p. 136.

45. Khushwant Singh, *op. cit.* p. 149.

46. *Satwant Kaur* p. 305.

CHAPTER 4

THE RULER IS VILLAIN

Villain, at times, in literature, is a necessary evil that helps hero and/or heroine in displaying their heroic qualities. And, villain, in some form, is present in Indian novel. Pyari Chand Mitra (1814-1887) who wrote under the *nom de plume* of Tek Chand Thakur in his novel *Alaler Gharer Dulal*[1] (*The Spoilt Child of Rich Family*), the first novel in Bengali, initially serialized in author's own magazine, *Masik Patra* and published in 1858, attempts to "show the pernicious efforts of allowing children to be improperly brought up."[2] Moti Lal is brought up under injurious set of circumstances and "represents a particular type of villainous character"[3] known for "his enthusiasm for the bottle"[4] and "promiscuous proclivity."[5] Before he "is rescued and miraculously converted by his virtuous younger brother Ram Lal"[6] to socially acceptable norms of life, his villainous conduct results in destroying the domestic bliss of the family he belongs to.

The entire focus in *Miratul Uroos*[7] (*The Bride's Mirror*), the first novel in Urdu, written by Deputy Nazir Ahmad (1831-1912) and puhlished in 1869, is on the mode of behaviour of two sisters married in two different families. Akbari the elder of the two was brought up in morally degenerated social milieu and hence a spoilt child, sowing the seed of discord brings about the break up of the joint family system. Whereas, in contrast the novelist presents Asghari, the younger one, as a model for 'Angel in the house'.

Sycophancy is under attack in *Priksaguru*[8], the first novel in Hindi, published in 1882. Sri Niwas Das (1850-97) its author, portrays the character of Lala Madan Mohan, a *raīs* of Delhi, who, in order to satisfy his morbid vanity, falls victim to sycophancy that makes him spendthrift and leads him to the blind alley of sexual lust and thereafter to insolvency. Now, it is a time of trial. In the process, Lala Madan Mohan learns to distinguish between sycophants like Munshi Chuni Lal, Master Shimbu Dyal, Pandit Parshotam Das and Hakim Ahmad Hussain and a friend like Brij Kishore Vakil. His wife, although, regularly neglected by him, too willingly, shares his miseries and stands by him at the time of trial. Madan Mohan learns from his own experience and experience alone is his *guru*. What the novelist wants to underline is that it is the vanity that is villainous and it interferes with the orderly life of one's family.

Chandu Menon's (1847-1899) *Indulekha*[9] published in 1889 "is held by all critics to be the first significant novel"[10] in Malayalm The clash between traditional authority and enlightenment serves as a device to weave a plot of *Indulekha.* Indulekha is engaged with Madhvan and latter picks up a quarrel with Panju Menon, the grandfather of Indulekha. Panju Menon gets so bitter that he tries to create conditions that Indulekha, instead, should marry a rich Nambudripad, who, in the words of the novelist, "represents the rich, licentious, proflgate unsteady Nambudripad so often found in Malabar".[11] And, Panju Menon fails in his *mission.* Indulekha and Madhvan, in the end, get married with each other. The happy ending is only delayed but not denied. Nambudri the villain is *used* by Panju Menon and the latter is in so case less villainous in his design.

All the four novels, analysed above, depict the domestic milieu of Indian life believed to have been affected by coming into contact with the British people. The new context, only, provided catalysis for the manifestation of villainous tendencies worked out in these novels. Before the novels in Indian languages were written the Britishers had already established themselves as an Empire. On the 2nd day of August 1858 the British Parliament had passed an Act which empowered British Crown to have sole authority in India and Lord Canning (r. 1858-62) took over the charge as a first Viceroy of India. An interaction between the Britishers and Indian people was inevitable and that, under the impact of the culture of ruling class, led to the formation of a new class in Indian society. Fashionable as it is to imitate the ruling elite, a section of Indian society started adjusting itself in the behaviourial pattern of the British Masters. This imitation on the part of section of Indian society resulted in disturbing an age-old domestic order that, by and large, forms the material of early Indian novel.

But, the problem is altogether different in the case of *Sundri*,[12] the first novel in Panjabi, published in the year 1898. *Sundri* is a political novel that depicts the political climate of mid 18th century Panjab. The novel begins with the abduction of a Hindu girl by a Mughal. Surasati (later on Sunder Kaur or Sundri) a young girl of eighteen and beautiful, whose marriage was due to be solemnized in a day or two is abducted by a Mughal. Bhai Vir Singh, the author, has used the expressions Turks and Mughals, in *Sundri*, interchangably. Clarifying the identity of the Chief or the Ruler he writes, that,

> In fact they were not Mughals, as their functioning had closed resemblance, so the people took them after the Mughals.[13]

Bhai Vir Singh invariably identifies the villain as Turk.[14]

The resemblance that exists between the Turk and Muslim, also, needs to be looked into. Muslims in *Sundrī* as compared to Turks/Mughals are referred to as brethren. What we learn about the Muslim is, that,

> (i) There was a small village thickly populated and inhabited by both the Hindus and Muslims'''[15].

> (ii) When a Sardar, after referring to a number of atrocities committed by Nawāb, declared his intention to punish him for his misdeeds, at once, two sweepers put a rope in his neck and hanged him from a tree. *Hindus and Muslims, both rejoiced* at seeing his body, thus, trembling.[16]

Obviously, Muslims were as much an integral part of the fraternity as the Hindus could be. All the three i.e. Hindus, Sikhs and Muslims, suffered at the hands of Turks, the Ruling Elite, of course, in varying degrees. But, why the Muslims suffered at the hands of Turks ? Were not the Muslims an integral part of the fraternity of Turks ? They were and they were not. Muslim, in those days, was one who not only professed and practised Islam but was also wedded to indigenous culture. Again, the Muslims, in this regard, consisted of two categories : (i) whose forefathers came from outside and had settled in India long ago and (ii) who himself (or his forefathers), at one time, belonged to the lower strata of Hindu society and was converted to Islam. Shaikh Farid (1175-1265) whose verses form the part of *Ādi Granth*, the scripture of the Sikhs, belonged to the first category. Waris Shah (1720/35-1798) who was Sayyid, the poet of *Heer*, a Panjabi classic and Bulle Shah (1680-1758) his close contemporary are also placed in this very category. Shah Hussain (1538-1599) the great *Sūfi* poet falls in the second category. All the four poets, though, belonged to different schools of Sufi thought and to different times, yet, were unanimous in condemning the politically dominant class-culture of their times not only in favour of their indigenous Panjabi culture, but also through pen and practice served the interests of common folk. Whereas Turks/Mughals, in those days professed Islam, but, they were not in the main stream of indigenous culture, instead, had a contempt for it. Islam constituted a common link between the Turks and Muslims and they belonged to one and the same religious fold alright, but the difference between them was much deeper as they were rooted in two different soils of culture. Muslims had their roots in Indian soil, whereas, Turks, naturally, continued with alien culture. It was always the cultural affinity that forged comfortable and cordial relations between the Hindus, Sikhs and Muslims of the Panjab.

Bhai Vir Singh's attack is on Turks/Mughals and not on Muslims. Turk is a Ruler and as a Ruler he has certain obligations towards the *ryot* or subject. One day a Muslim lady[17] with one small child in her laps and two holding with her fingers, in rags and starving, came to Sham Singh. He asked her as to what had brought her there. She told Sham Singh that she had come to him for justice and narrated her a tale of woe to him. That her husband was courtier of the local Chief. One day, her husband, in the state of drunkeness, fell out with the *Nawāb,* who got him killed then and there and looted all their property and reduced her to begging. On hearing about the plight of destitute Muslim lady Sham Singh helped her with some money. But, a certain *brāhmaṇa,* who was sitting by the side of Sham Singh did not approve of Sham Singh's kind gesture as the latter had shown sympathy for *malechan.* Now, Sham Singh apprised the *brāhamaṇa* of their crusade against the Mughals, saying ;

> Listen *miśra ji* ! we are not prone to partisanship, neither we are inimical to anybody, what to talk of Hindus and Muslims. our *Satgurūs* never nursed an ill-will against anybody, we practise equanimity towards the whole humanity. We are committed to uproot injustice and must weigh things properly. At present, the Rulers who are committing atrocities, we are to set them right and to set them right is to uproot atrocities.
>
> *Brāhamaṇa* spoke. Then why do you kill Turks ? You take refuge in them.
>
> Sham Singh : Pandit Ji !
>
> We are not against Turks or Pathana because they are Muslims and neither we are destroying their rule being prompted by ill-will against them, we are bent upon destroying the rule of Mughals because being Kings they inflict sufferings on their subject, they do not practise justice. They accept bribe and in turn execute innocent people. They get revenue but hardly protect the life and property of their subject. They interfere with other's religions and forcibly convert them. This is a sin. This is not the ethic of a King. This is why we are committed to uproot the rule based on injustice. We are not against any caste or creed......[18].

Here, Sham Singh seems to be a victim to illusion-an Illusion of Age—rooted in widely acclaimed but least practised theory of Divine Right of Kingship[19], that raised our hopes unlikely to be fulfilled. Sham Singh is, undoubtedly, presented as a model of Sikh tradition What follows from Sham Singh's views is that there is absolutely no opposition to caste and creed in Sikh tradition, it is opposed to cruelty and injustice. One thing more and which is quite fundamental also emerges that the Sikh tradition approves of the institution of kingship and was opposed only to rule of injustice in favour of the Rule of Law. This interpretation, if accepted, means that the Sikh tradition which is ideologically based on *Gurbāṇi* or teachings of Gurus, aims at merely reforming the prevailing system. Reform seeks improvement within the framework of prevailing system, whereas, revolution stands to demolish the entire prevailing system and build up a new system, altogether. Whether the Sikh tradition is reformatory or revolutionary in its approach, this proposition has already been analysed, carefully and dispassionately, and characterized as revolutionary, thus, identifying the true nature of the Sikh psyche.

Bhai Vir Singh the novelist, through Sham Singh, his spokesman, has levelled certain allegations against the Rulers of the time. The novelist too comments upon the general tone of administration, as ;

> Hindu parents would hardly allow their daughters to move out in these hards days of life and kept their daughters and daughters-in-laws like the prisoners. The beautiful woman, wealth and pelf could hardly be the possession of a Hindu.[20]

So, the Rulers are debauch and dacoits. Once, a certain *khatri*, while telling his tale of woe to Sundri, told her that, finally, the Mughal offered him to free him but with a condition "if he would handover his wife to him."[21]

Another significant villainous trait dominantly present in the psyche of the Turk, the Ruler, is his enthusiasm for proselytization of Hindus and Sikhs to Islam. Proselytization as has been practised in the sphere of religion consists of two kinds : peaceful and coercive. The system of peaceful proselytization among the Sikhs (like the one which Mahavira and the Buddha practised in the sixth century B.C.) as against the coercive one, of the Turks, continues to be in practise. The Sikhs are, mainly, opposed to the practise of coercive proselytization by the Turks. Why do the Turks, the Rulers, practise coercive proselytization ? The simple answer is to expand their range of power. Bertrand Russell (1872-1970) in one of the chapters entitled, "Creeds as Sources of Power" of his book, *Power* (1938) has made certain observations quite useful for understanding the attempts made at forcible proselytization. The Turks both as a religious and political community were, undoubtedly, in minority. To add into their political power they made use of their professed (if not practised) religion. "The power of community" writes Bertrand Russell, "depends not only upon its numbers and its economic resources and its technical capacity, but also upon its beliefs."[22] So, the common beliefs, dear to the members of a community, bring them together. This togetherness constituting doctrinal uniformity provides power to the community, that, at times, converts the community into a fanatical creed. "The classical example of power through fanaticism" observes Russell, "is the rise of Islam"[23]. The Turks were practising the same fanaticism, manifested through forcible conversion of Hindus and Sikhs into Islam. Believing that it could help them to gain more power over the people.

The socalled religious ceremony of converting infidels or *Kāfirs* to Islam, following the semitic tradition, was always performed in public with a view to demonstrate their strength and spread terror among the Rebels and Loyalists, alike. Bhai Vir Singh has narrated one such episode in *Sundri.* The necessary arrangements are made in the main mosque crowded with horrified people. A close palanquin accompanied by a man, who is hand-cuffed, arrives. The man is wearing a dirty *Kacchā* (underwear) and a dirty shirt, and a small turban on his head and one can see the scattered hair through it. He has a dismal face but his eyes are red with anger. A woman with a *burqā* (veil) got out of the palanquin and both of them entered the mosque and were made to sit facing the *mullā* (parish-priest) especially invited for the occasion. The horrified people are watching the *show* with terror-stricken looks when the *mullā* said :

> Balwant Singh ! Do you willingly accept Islam ?
>
> Balwant Singh : I shall too willingly accept death.[24]

Mullā looks towards *Nawāb* and says that, "he is a big *mūzī* (noxious) he will not surrendeı this way, either he should bc killed or forcibly......"[25].

> *Nawāb* : Yes, the latter (course) is better and I don't want to kill thc brother of this *mahārū* (Beauty).
>
> *Mullā* : Is *hajām* (barber) present ?
>
> *Barber* : Yes. I am present, Sir.
>
> *Mullā* : Come here and cut his hair.[26]

While talking about the reported programme, prior to actually holding the public ceremony, one soldier expressed his heartful satisfaction to another saying that, "watching these Sikhs being converted to Islam in itself is *Swāb* (reward)."[27] But, the *Allāh* wished otherwise. Bhai Vir Singh has quite vividly described how the cyclone appeared that was converted into a band of soliders, who killed some of the soliders lined up in the bazar, out side the mosque, and picked up the chained Balwant Singh and Surasati, placed them on the horseback and fled away, ultimately freeing both of them from the clutches of *Nawāb* and *mullā*.

Merciless killing and torture were some of the other measures the Rulers frequently made use of for suppressing Sikhs the Rebels. Bhai Vir Singh has given the account of such abominable deeds of the Rulers (or their allies) in his novels. In general, after the attack of Nadir Shah in 1739 Khan Bahadur continued with the massacre of the Sikhs. The *Caudhries* or Chiefs of villages were instructed to get the Sikh killed, whenever and whereever he was found and confiscate his property. The roving columns started their operations, in the areas, for the elimination of the Sikhs. The informers had had their days. Whosoever helped in arresting the Sikhs was amply rewarded A good number of Sikhs, as a result of that, left their homes and took shelter in the forests. The Sikh women and Sikh children were tortured in number of ways. Some of these atrocious measures taken by the Rulers, the novelist has enlisted as under ;

> (i) ......These Sikhs were tortured by tieing them on the revolving wheel. In Lahore the wells were filled with the heads of the Sikhs and thereby raised the *mīnār* (minaret).[28]
>
> (ii) ... When the persuation failed to make them forsake their [Sikhs] religion then, at a signal from Mir Mannu,......these *Jallāds* (hangmen) wrapped the Sikhs in the cotton in the same manner in which the *poorbias* make idols of Hanuman on the eve of the Holi festival. The hands and the feet of the Sikhs were tied to a distant peg to prevent them from moving. Just as oil is offered to a bridegroom at the time of his riding the mare. Similarly oil was sprinkled on the Sikhs.......[29]
>
> (iii) ....
>
> Snatching children from their mothers,
> And, willfully right in their faces,
> In the air they were thrown,
> Pulling roots, thus, their own
> Many were taken on the spear,
> And killed in a way barbaric sheer.[30]

Not only the Rulers but their allies too were in no way less enthusiastic in inflicting inhuman injuries on the Sikhs. Lakhpat Rai was one of the such ally. His brother, Jaspat Rai, in alliance with the Rulers was also working against the Sikhs. He was iustrumental in conspiring the arrest of Bhai Mani Singh. The Sikhs in order to avenge the death of Bhai Mani Singh killed Jaspat Rai. Lakhpat Rai went to *Nawāb* of Lahore and complained that the Sikhs had killed his brother and to avenge his brother, he pledged before the *Nawāb* that he must, if he is a true *khatri*, eliminate the entire Sikh community. The *Nawāb*, obviously, gave his consent and put the army and artillery at his disposal. One day Lakhpat Rai, while on horse-back, was roaming in Lahore. On seeing a Sikh family he exclaimed that, "How is it that the Sikhs are still moving in Lahore in daylight" ?[31] He ordered the soliders to catch hold of the Sikh and on enquiring about the fault, Lakhpat Rai told him, that :

> It is a grave offence to be a Sikh. Now either you give up your religion or face death.[32]

Lakhpat Rai tried his utmost to convert Bhai Harkirat Singh and his family to Islam but of no use. Then Lakhpat Rai ordered that :

> Oh Solidiers ! Kill the Sikh and take his wife and son to Maulvi Jan Beg, to convert them to Islam.[33]

On hearing these words Bhai Sahib's wife caught hold of his son from the neck and told her husband, that "let her press his throat and you press her throat and they are very likely to kill you. Hurry up, don't delay, it is time to save the honour or our religion."[34] The child was killed first then the woman followed by the Sikh.

The atrocities committed against the Sikhs had one and only one objective, namely, to paralize the rebellious spirit of the Sikhs.

References and Notes :

1. Braijendra Nath Bandyopadhyay and Sainikacita Das (Eds.) *Alaler Gharer Dulal*, 1940-47.

2-6. Jayanti Chattopadhyay, *The Villain in the Nineteenth Century Bengali Literature*, p. 2

7. Its nineteenth edition was published by Munshi Naval Kishore, Lucknow, in April, 1949.

   Miratul Uroos, according to Ashfaq Ahmad Azmi was also translated in other Indian languages e.g. Bengali, Marathi, Gujrati, Kashmiri and Panjabi.
   See : Ashfaq Ahmad Azmi, *Nazir Ahmad : Shakhsiyat Aur Karname*. p. 140.
   For the English trnalation of *Miratul Uroos*
   See : G. E. Ward (Trs) *The Bride's Mirror*, 1953.

8. Shri Krishan Lal (Ed.) *Sri Niwas Das Granthavali*, 1953,

9. Chandu Menon, *Indulekha*, 1889.

10. R.E. Asher, "Three Novelists of Kerala" in *The Novel in India* edited by T.W. Clark, p. 208.

11. W. Dumergue translated *Indulekha* which was published in 1890 (Reprinted 1965). This reference is from a letter by the author to the translator at p. xvii.

12. There is but a passing reference to the bad effects of western education (*Satwant Kaur* p. 88) and lust for the English ladies (*Bijay Singh* p. 148) among the Sikhs.

13. Bhai Vir Singh, *Sundri*, p. 10n; See p. 40.

14. *Ibid* pp. 8-12, 16, 21, 23. Some of the very significant references are as under :

    (i) When Balwant Singh, a neo-convert to Sikh faith, after the abduction of Surasti later on Sunder Kaur or Sundri) his sister, brings, her back from the captivity of the ruler to the parents, rather than expressing their admiration on his heroic act, he is rebuked, instead, thus :

What have you done damned fellow ! Will the *Turk* forgive us now. The moment he discovers that our son is a Sikh, he will doom all of us...p. 8.

(ii) And both the sister and brother [Surasati and Balwant Singh] were taken into captivity by the group of *Turks*, to suffer. p. 12.

(iii) Bhai Balwant Singh and his sister [Surasati] are in the captivity in Doaba and on Friday they will be forcibly converted as *Turks*. p. 16, see pp. 34, 36

Also, the invaders were contemptuously called *mallecha* pp. 34-35

15. *Ibid* p. 1.
16. *Ibid* p. 47
17. *Ibid* p. 42
18. *Ibid* pp. 43-44; see. p. 4 : see : *Bijay Singh* p. 50 (same idea)
19. See Appendix B *The Divine Right of Kingship*
20. *Sundri* pp. 2-3
21. *Ibid* p. 33
22. Bertrand Russell, *Power* p. 99
23. Idem
24. *Sundri* p. 17
25. *Idem*
26. *Ibid* p. 18
27. *Ibid* p. 15
28. *Ibid* pp. 72, 94
29. *Bijay Singh* p. 81
30. *Ibid* p. 92

31-32. *Sundri* p. 57

33. *Ibid* p. 58
34. *Idem.*

For similar atrocities committed against Sajjan Singh's family see : *Bijay Singh* pp. 22-23
Also see : *Bijay Singh* p. 37

CHAPTER 5

THE SIKH IDEAL

Prior to the commencement of trilogy, the *Khālsā*, to steer an armed revolt against the barbarous State, had already been created and Banda Bahadur had already fought and sacrificed his life and the lives of his dear ones for the Holy Cause. Three major characters, namely, Sundri's brother Balwant Singh, Sundri and Bijay Singh are newly converted into the *Khālsā Panth* under the spell of high ideals set forth and promoted by Guru Gobind Singh. Balwant Singh, (whose Hindu name is not made known) son of Shama, a rich man, became Sikh as a result of being in the company of the Sikhs.[1] When Balwant Singh after rescuing Surasati, his sister, from thr captivity of Turk, was not welcomed by his parents he took his sister along with him. Surasati used to listen about the teaching of Sikh religion from her brother and had inwardly changed, accordingly. Surasati was reciting *Japji*, while sitting on pyre she had herself prepared in order to save her honour, when Balwant Singh reached and saved her. As she had heard the stories of valour of the Sikhs this idea continuously haunted her that "Why don't women also fight in defence of their *Dharma*" ?[2] and she resolved to be one like her brother. At one stage Surasati expressed her views to Sham Singh, the great Sikh Warrior, that,

> I am no more interested in *Grahast mārg* (household life) and my husband has deserted me. It was his

> duty to protect (my honour) when he shirked from that. Now, I don't want to indulge in it again, when my Guru has saved me (from that rut). I wish to serve the *Khālsā* and, thus, make my life fruitful...
>
> ....It does not behove me not to spend the days of my life in the cause of *Dharma*, when my brother has put his life at the stake for protecting the *Dharma*. Kindly give me your blessings so that I recite *Bāṇi*, remember *Nām* and render service.[3]

Surasati's request was granted, she was baptized and given the name of Sunder Kaur (follwing the practice of getting first letter from the *Ādi Granth*) later on popularized as Sundri.

Bijay Singh (whose Hindu name was Ram Lal) is a son of Churh Mal, renown money lender of Lahore and government official, and himself a government employee got converted into Sikh-fold. These conversions, as opposed to the forcible conversions[4] into the Religion of the Rulers, referred to in the trilogy were voluntary[5] in nature and earned the wrath of both the parents and the Rulers. The parents of these newly converted, by and large, lamented their children's folly and did express their grief. Bhai Vir Singh, while summing up the sentiments of the affected parents, writes :

> In those days when some one in the family used to become Sikh (*Khālsā*) the parents would take it worse than the death and generally discarded their sons. In case some one would ask as to 'how many sons do you have ?' then they would say 'I had five sons; one died and one got converted as a Sikh, now there are three by the Grace of God.[6]

Utter disgust and annoyance of the parents over the *unbecoming* behaviour of their childern, also finds expression in direct manner. Look at the anguish of Bijay Singh's father when the latter bursts at him, saying :

> O ye, accursed fellow, I wish you had never been born. It would have been better if either you or your mother had died before your birth. May you be destroyed for having driven me to these straits at this age.[7]

Bulaki Shah in *Satwant Kaur* also expressed his indignation in a letter addressed to his sons, Mansa Singh and Sukha Singh, newly converted into *Khālsā Panth*.[8]

Out of the five K's obligatory for the *Khālsā*, the most significant, at the moment, is *keś* (unshorn hair). It is also said that when the Tenth Guru through his *hukamnāmās*[9] asked the *Saṅgat* to come to Anandpur, he also instructed them to come with long beards and unshorn hair. This emblem is very special in the sense that it has become a distinguishing feature of the Sikh community. There are some specific references to the *keśās* in the trilogy that need to be analysed.

In *Sundri*,[10] Bhai Vir Singh, on the basis of informations provided by Ratan Singh Bhangu, in his chronicle *Panth Prakaś* (1880), has referred to one Sukha Singh, whose parents dreading the wrath of Turks, cut his hair while he was unconscious. Sukha Singh could not stand his humiliation and decided to commit suicide when one Sikh advised him better to die as a martyr. Then, Sukha Singh joined the *jathā* of Sardar Sham Singh, got baptized and fought number of battles in pursuance of the Sikh Ideal. Bijay Singh too joined the Order of *Khālsā* and was under the obligation to preserve the sanctity of an emblem of *Khālsā*, but his attachment to the *keśās*, somehow, seems to have taken the form of obsession that leads him astray from the *Panth* Bijay Singh's philosophy of *keśās* is revealed while in conversation with his mother and we reproduce the relevant part verbatim, as under :

> Mother : My son ! These *Keśās* that you are keeping are causing much anxiety......When you were living with us you did perform all the rituals of the Sikh tradition and none questioned you at all. It was all under the garb of secrecy and nothing untoward could happen.[11]

... ...

Son : Mother ! tell me the way through which no damage is caused to my sentiments and it drives you out from your miseries, as well.

Mother : Abandon the *keśās* and the company of the Sikhs, look like your father and do whatever you like, but stay at home.

Son : Oh my mother ! what have you said. You want me to live double standard of life......I adore *keśās* more than I value my life......*My keśās* are the token of love of my Guru......I shall prefer dying than doing away with them [12]

The mother pressed upon Bijay Singh so much that he became emotional and said :

> Mother ! I can do this much for you that I stay in *Caubārā* (secluded place) and spend the days of my life there. I shall not communicate with any body and shall live the life of solitude that would do no harm to you. But I cannot imagine the kind of life devoid of my *Dharma*.[13]

So, Bijay Siagh prefers to live in *caubārā*—a secluded life—to doing away with the *Keśās*. He thinks that his decision helps him to undo with the double standard of life. He hardly finds any difficulty in thus observing the commands of his Guru. He is sure of following the path shown by the Guru. It hardly causes any damage to his *Dharma*. Bijay Singh finds the solution of all these problems in just having unshorn hair. Guru's command to keep the unshorn hair meant to '*raṇa mein at joojh marṇā*.[14] - 'to fight and die in the battle-field', and it was certainly not to retire to *caubārā*. Bijay Singh altogether overlooked the ideological aspect of unshorn hair. He, in fact, got slipped and the whole matter shifted from character to dogma and, thus, the Sikh Ideal was diluted, as if the unshorn hair were the be all and end all of the Guru's command. It would not be out of place to point out, at this stage, that this kind of philosophy of unshorn hair was, in fact, the ideal of the Singh Sabha movement. The Sikhs could bargain with the Government only in the capacity of a community distinct from other contemporary religious communities such as Hindu and Muslim communities. The unshorn hair could and did work well. The titles, such as Rai Sahib, Khan Sahib and Sardar Bahadur, conferred by the British Government, hold testimony to the above stated fact. These measures adopted by the Government provided vicarious satisfaction to the people belonging to different religious communities and the Government, in turn, successfully manipulated the loyalities of these people.

In spite of the fact that Bijay Singh's mother was fully satisfied with the proposal but his father did not agree to it as the *Nawāb* had come to know about Bijay Singh's conversion to Sikhism. The father could not afford to displease the *Nawāb* and, thus, forced Bijay Singh to leave.

The *Khālsā* fought against the coercive authorities of the State, alright, but what matters is the manner in which they fought. The *Khālsā* derived inspiration from the Gurus, such as, Guru Nanak,[15] Guru Tegh Bahadur[16] and Guru Gobind Singh[17] and Sikh martyrs like *Cār Sāhib Zāde*[18] (four sons of Guru Gobind Singh), Bhai Mani Singh,[19] Bhai Taru Singh.[20] Subheg Singh,[21] Shahid Baba Deep Singh,[22] and Banda Bahadur.[23] Mata Sahib Devan[24] (wife of Guru Gobind Singh) and Mai Bhago[25] are also remembered with reverence as they also inspired the *Khālsā* to fight for the common man. But the significant thing here is that *Khālsā* while deriving moral force from the Sikh heritage looked more towards Guru Gobind Singh and to those who subscribed to the cult of sword and thus died for the cause identified by the Guru. And it was quite in conformity with the then Sikh Ideal. A living religion is a growing religion and Sikhism is one such religion. Growth is effected through interaction and alive response to the situations. The growth of Sikh movement from pacifist in nature to militant *Khālsā* was not a sudden jump, it was rather, an alive response to the oppressive mearures adopted by the Rulers, aimed at eliminating the Sikh community imbibing rebellious spirit. It was in this context that Guru Gobind Singh created *Khālsā* , apart from other things, adhering to the cult of sword. Guru Gobind Singh in *Zafarnama* (1707) an epistle letter written in Persian and addressed to Emperor Aurangzeb, glorifying an act of violence as righteous act stated that :

> *Cu kār az hamā hīlate dar guzaśt*
> *halāl ast būrdan ba śamsir dast*
> When all the means are rendered vain
> It is righteous to draw the sword.[26]

The Guru, thus, in so many words underlined his philosophy of violence revolutionary in its contents.

The *Khālsā* also remained wedded to *Gurbāṇi*,[27] *Adi*

Granth,[28] the latter now adorned as a Living Guru under the command of Guru Gobind Singh and made use of *ardāsa*[29] (prayer) during the 'Term of Trial'. *Jaikāre*[30] such as '*Gurbar akāl*' '*Sat Siri akāl*' and *Wāhegurū ji kā Khālsa, wāhegurū ji ki fateh*', too prompted them to imbibe martial spirit. The cause, therefore, was noble and it brought into being the Saint-Soldier. The *Khālsā* was destined to fight againsl the Evil manifested in different forms at different points of time in the history. The *Khālsā* waged a Holy War against Zakariya Khan and Mir Mannu etc. because the latter had joined hands with Satan.

The *Khālsā* during the period of turmoil made forests their home and frequently used the sweet roots and the fruits of the forests as their food[31] and inspite of the fact that neither they had any land nor money and were bereft of any friendly help[32] from any quarter and still imbibed high spirits (*cardi kalā*). There was absolutely no ambiguity so far their mission was concerned. The *Khālsā* looted the booty[33] and treasury[34] but never harmed the innocent[35] people and advocated full respect for women and at one time rescued 2100[36] Hindu women from the captivity of Nadir Shah. Their only desire was to get their Homeland free from the yoke of foreign rule,[37] as they were convinced that Panjab was their Homeland[38] and were sure that one day the Sikhs shall be the Master of their Homeland.[39] As regard the means of acquiring Home-Rule the Sikhs would not beg for it, rather, shall have it by means of sword.[40]

We have earlier referred to the opinions of Sant Singh Sekhon, Surinder Singh Dusanjh and Amarjot Sekhon in connection with the character of Sikh movement as protrayed by Bhai Vir Singh in the trilogy. These opinions need to be looked into. Sekhon fails to find economic and political contents in the struggle against the atrocities committed by the Mughal ruling class.[41] Dusanjh calls it "the war of peasantry and labour-class"[42] and Amarjot opines that it is depiction of "the life of middle class shop-keepers as a prototypal of the Sikh movement.[43] For Sekhon, it is merely a "religious protest." Let us know what the *Manual of Fundamentals of Marxism-Leninism* has to say about the religious protest. "The Sikh uprisings in India (17th-18th Centuries)"[44] in this Manual are adjudged as "peasant uprisings."[45] Dusanjh is aware of the Marxian position. But, he looks to the stock the *Khālsā* came from. The same is true in the case of Amarjot. After joining the Order of *Khālsā* one is no other than the *Khālsā*. Therefore, it was neither the war of peasantry and labour class nor that of the middle class shop-keepers. It was a war of the *Khālsā* to provide an alternative of egalitarian society (*Khālsā Panth*) as against the existing one based on inequality.

Bhai Vir Singh has, one may misinterpret, narrowed down the concept of egalitarian society by substituting it with the 'Sikh egalitraian society'. The last words of Sundri were :

> "Brothers ! when you become the Rulers, don't look down upon any Singh ....[46]

In fact, the Sikh revolution did not cross the frontiers of the Order of *Khālsā*. The character of Sundri is cast in this very pattern.

The *Khālsā*, at times, did take revenge[47] against their enemies – the Rulers and their allies—but most important characteristic that emerges is their Compassion invariably followed by the latter's ingratitude which is vividly described in the trilogy. While on the way back from the village, cacompained by Dharm Kaur, after purchasing salt for the *laṅgar*, Sundri heard the cries of some person and searched for it and found that a young man was bleeding and had on his shoulder a wound of a sword besides minor injuries. The blood was flowing like a fountain and his face was growing pale. Both the ladies helped the wounded young man. Sundri thought if they left him there he would certainly die. Sundri was in the state of ambivlence; if she takes him to the forest—resort of the Sikhs—firstly, it was difficult to carry him there, secondly, he is Turk and her brother would not approve of her step. But, ultimately, both the ladies resolved that he should be taken over there and rendered proper service as that was the demand of Sikhism. When Sundri brought the whole matter in the notice of her brother and Sham Singh, the *jathedār*, both felt little annoyed with Sundri and made her to understand that, 'yes, Compassion *is* our *dharma* but time is such that we must remain vigilant so far the Turks are concerned and we should not expect any good in return from them.''[48]

The young Turk was given hospitality and medical treatment and after his complete recovery from illness as desired, he was allowed to leave the place.

The Turk proved as predicted. Sundri, one day, was returning from the same village to the resort when on the way the same Turk with the help of armed soldiers made Sundri, once again, the captive of the *Nawāb*, who had earlier got her abducted.[49]

In *Satwant Kaur*,[50] on enquiry as to how such a brave lady happened to be a prisoner, Satwant Kaur tells *Amīr Sāhib* that one day his officer, while riding on his horseback fell into the blind well. She saw him falling and with the help of village-folk got him out of the well and served him with medical treatment for about eight or ten days. After he recovered he left for Ludhiana and from there, one day, he sent a message to her father telling him that his wife was greatly beholden to her and she desired to see her. Her father declined to send her there. After ten days or so he alongwith his wife came to their home. She felt little attachment for his wife. One day she went to meet her in the tent. He imprisoned her and took her to his place. That lady, in fact, was not his wife. He forced her to marry him. Next day *Amīr* moved towards his home-land and he was asked to leave ahead. In this turmoil she was left behind and on seeing her tied *Amīr's* soldiers took her as slave. She was taken captive and was sold there like many others.

Bhai Vir Singh has identified ingratitude as a characteristic feature of the Ruler and his allies.

Again, it is stated in *Satwant Kaur*[51] that during the battle between Paṭhan soldiers of Abdali and the Sikhs, fought at Barnala the then Capital of Patiala, a good number of soldiers from both the sides were wounded. The Sikh women (including Satwant Kaur) rendered medical service to the wounded soldiers irrespective of being the Sikh or the Paṭhan. This noble gesture of the Sikh women remainds us of Bhai Kanahiya[52] (1647-1718 circa), the founder of *Sewa Panth*, the Sikh sect known for its sacrifice of ego in the service of humanity. Bhai Kanahaiya was born in the year 1647 (circa) at Village Sodhre, district Gujranwala, now in Pakistan. His father was a merchant who used to supply food etc. to the Imperial army. He is said to have imbibed the spirit of Compassion right in his childhood. Bhai Kanahaiya happened to visit Anandpur to seek blessings of Guru Tegh Bahadur and became his devotee. Thereafter after the martyrdom of Guru Tegh Bahadur, Bhai Kanahaiya served at the feet of Guru Gobind Singh, who was immensely pleased with his Compassionate heart and instructed him not to take *amrit* and become a saint-soldier, but to do service to the people.

The hill-chiefs in league with Imperial army of Emperor Aurangzeb, attacked Anandpur to defeat Guru Gobind Singh and thus to destroy his growing popularity and patronage among his followers. A pitch battle ensued in which both the sides suffered heavy causualities. Compassion displayed, in this battle, made Kanahaiya immortal. He served with water the wounded and dying soldiers without any discrimination of foe or friend. Bhai Kanahaiya's conduct hurt the feelings of the Sikh soldiers and they made a petition against this before the Guru. The Guru called Bhai Kanahaiya to explain. Bhai Kanahaiya reminded the Guru of his teaching 'to look all human beings alike.' (*mānas ki jāt sab eko pecānbo*). The Guru approved of the conduct, showered blessings on him and gave him an ointment, in addition to serving water, to dress and heal the wounds of the soldiers. The Guru clarified, yes, the soldier is an enemy when fighting against us, but no more an enemy when wounded or killed. Bhai Kanahaiya is very rightly revered as a symbol of Compassion.

There is, yet, one more dimension of Compassion associated with the person of Guru Tegh Bahadur. When the *brāhamins* of Kashmir in scarch for the saviour, approached Guru Tegh Bahadur, writes Trilochan Singh, that :

> He [the Guru] did not believe in idolatory. He did not believe in the sacred thread and frontol marks. He did not believe in *Brāhamanism*; he and his predecessors had been preaching against it for two hundred years............The woeful tales of the *Brāhamins* moved Guru Tegh Bahadur to profound pity [*sic*] and compassion. Their sorrow became his personal sorrow.[53]

Trilochan Singh has rightly hinted at Compassion displayed by the Guru irrespective of his ideology, but seems to have utterly failed in perceiving what exactly Compassion is? when he clubs Compassion with pity. When we pity a man we look down upon him, whereas, Compassion springs when we see one Life breathing in all living beings. How does it happen ? Energy, when manifests through dark passions such as *kām*, *karodha*, *loba*, *moha* and *ahṁkāra* etc. is transformed through *nām-simran,* in Sikh tradition, and thus ennobled is called Compassion, though operates at different levels *is* unconditional and unmixed in contents.

Celebacy is another characteristic feature of the Sikhs that finds ample evidence in the trilogy. Sundri[54] was abducted number of times by the Mughal Chief desiring to dishonour her by sexual assault and/or converting her into Islam and she successfully foiled his attempts at all times. Satwant Kaur[55] too was induced and forced to submit in the similar manner by the *Amīr* of Kabul, but she managed to escape the evil designs of *Amīr*. Sheel Kaur[56] (wife of Bijay Singh) also became target of Mir Mannu's similar intentions and she did not dwindle and kept up the integrity of her character in the true spirit of Sikh tradition.

Not only the Sikh women but the Sikh male characters are also portrayed having adopted celebacy as norm of life. Bijay Singh, besides the valour, is cast in the pattern of celebacy highly eulogised in the Sikh ethos. Murad Begam also referred to as Mughlani Begam, now the widow of Mir Mannu, notorious for licentious nature, who once tried to seduce Bhikhari Khan.[57] the *wazīr* and on accouut of refusal to oblige her, she got him killed, also made advances to tempt Bijay Singh, during the period when along with his wife and son he was captive in the royal palace. For proper appreciation of the said episode, better if we listen to what Begam proposed and how Bijay Singh declined her offer, in the words of the author, as :

Begam : I have committed no sin by suggesting a marriage which is a sacred relationship.

Bijay Singh......As far as I am concerned I am already......Also I shall never accept Islam come what may......

Begam : ......Have you ever known a woman begging for marriage. This is an indication of my deep love for you......

Bijay Singh : I cannot enter into such a relationship because I am a Singh......[58]

Begam was hurt but she resisted to repeat the story of Bhikhari Khan, which had already exposed her in the eyes of the public, Bijay Singh came out victorious in the battle in which to safeguard his celebacy, he had put his life at stake.

Bhai Vir Singh intended to protray the characters of Sundri and Bijay Singh and others to serve as models of the Sikh Ideal for his contemporary and his models are quite defective in some measures. Sundri's contempt for *Grahsat* (household life) is a gross violation of norms of life set by the Gurus. Bijay Singh's commitment to his mother to stay in *Caubārā* in preference to shaving his hair off, at least, once, puts him in a questionable position. Though, later on, his conduct exonerates him, fully.

References and Notes

1. *Sundri* : p. 6.
2, *Ibid* : p. 11.
3. *Ibid* : p. 25.
4. *Ibid* : pp 14-18; *Bijay Singh* : pp. 63, 64, 66, 67, 81, 88-89, 91: *Satwant Kaur* : pp. 21-22, 181-182, 229.

5. *Sundri* p. 47

6. *Ibid* : p. 6. n; Hari Ram Gupta, *History of the Sikhs* Vol. II, p. 41 : "If anybody enquired of a Hindu woman how many sons she had, she would reply that she had three sons, but one of them had become a Sikh. Thereby she meant that the converted one should bc considered among the dead".

7. Davindar Singh Duggal (Trs.) *Bijay Singh* p. 7.

8. *Satwant Kaur* : p. 206

9. Bhai Santokh Singh, *Sūraj Prakāś*, iii, 21. Quoted in Teja Singh and Ganda Singh, *A short History of the Sikhs* p. 69.

10. *Sundri* : pp. 73-74; also see : *Bijay Singh* : p. 20.

11. *Bijay Siugh* : p 8

12. *Ibid* p. 10

13. *Ibid* p. 16 But later on she revised her views and started adoring *keśās*, see : p. 35

14. *Dasam Granth* (*Caṇdicaritar I*) p. 99

15. *Bijay Singh* : p. 72; *Satwant Kaur* : pp. 75, 77, 81, 87, 141, 143, 271, 20.

16. *Sundrī* : p. 8.

17. *Sundri* : pp. 15, 24, 28, 75, 77, 115, 124; *Bijay Singh* : pp. 20, 31, 56, 81-82, 153; *Satwant Kaur* : pp. 1-2, 99, 198, 250, 253-256, 274, 287.

18. *Sundri* : p. 26

19. *Sundri* : pp 27, 60; *Bijay Singh* : pp. 9, 69, 90, 125; *Satwant Kaur* : p. 203.

20. *Bijay Singh* : pp. 13, 86 *Satwant Kaur* : p. 203.

21. *Satwant Kaur* : p. 203

22. *Sundri* : pp. 78, 85, *Bijay Singh* p. 156

23. *Satwant Kaur* : pp. 97, 197.

24. *Sundri* : pp. 28, 48, 126.

25. *Sundri* : p. 26.

26. *Zafarnama* verse —46

27. *Sundri* : pp. 7, 27; *Bijay Singh* : pp. 32, 35, 43, 61, 74, 78, 105, 113, 133, 137, 139; *Satwant Kaur* : pp. 11, 29, 32, 72, 76, 87-88, 94, 100-101, 103-104, 107, 109, 113, 115-118, 123-125, 127, 140-141, 148, 176, 194, 206, 213, 216, 270, 283-284.

28. *Sundri* : pp. 13, 28; *Bijay Singh* : p. 22, *Satwant Kaur*: p. 127.

29. *Satwant Kaur* : pp. 30, 125-126, 137, 172, 194, 270, 284-285. For exhaustive analysis of *Ardāsa*, see Jaswant Singh Neki, *Ardās-Roop, Darśan and Abhias.*

30. *Sundri* : pp. 17, 21; *Bijay Siugh* : p. 112: *Satwant Kaur* : pp. 252, 254.

31. *Bijay Singh* : p. 41; *Satwant Kaur* p. 132-

32. *Bijay Singh* : p. 119.

33. *Sundri* : p. 99

34. *Ibid* : p. 22

35. *Idem* : p. 22

36. *Ibid* : p. 126; *Satwant Kaur* : p. 165
See *Sundri* : p. 40n. and pp. 136ff.

37. *Sundri* : p. 99

38. *Satwant Kaur* : 17

39. *Sundri* : pp. 83, 126-127; *Bijay Singh* : p. 55, *Satwant Kaur* : p. 217.

40. *Bijay Singh* : p. 146

41-43. See chapter 1, Reference Nos. 32-35

44-45. *Manual of Fundamentals of Marxism-Leninism* pp. 130-131.

46. *Sundri* p. 127; Jagjit Singh *The Sikh Revolution*. p. 212.
47. *Sundri* : pp. 46-47, *Bijay Singh* : 114
48. *Sundri* : pp. 47-50
49. *Ibid* : pp. 50-51
50. *Satwant Kaur* : pp. 18-19
51. *Ibid* : p. 306, See : *Sundri* pp. 106-107
52. Satbir Singh, *Puratan Itihasak Jiwinian*
53. Trilochan Singh, *Guru Tegh Bahadur : Prophet and Martyr* pp. 297-298
54. *Sundri* : pp. 7, 8, 16-18, 51-54, 76-77
55. *Satwant Kaur* : pp. 20-21
56. *Bijay Singh* : p. 99
57. *Ibid* : p. 126
58. Davinder Singh Duggal, (Trs.) *Bijay Singh* pp. 128-129

CHAPTER 6

THE RISE OF BRITISH EMPIRE

During the period when the trilogy was published i.e. 1898-1900, Lord Elgin II (r. 1894-99) and Lord Curzon (r. 1899-1905) were the Viceroys of British India. The Britishers had been sovereign for full four decades since the passing of Act of British Parliament in 1858 which terminated the rule of East India Company. The developments taken during these four decades and the way Bhai Vir Singh responded to these developments do serve as a background for understanding the Sikh psyche that was taking shape in the hands of Singh Sabha movement, whose spokesman our author was.

As the trilogy is conceived in the background of historical period called 'Decline of the Mughal Empire' and written and published during the British Rule that marked the qualitative change, as compared to the earlier system of the near past, in the set-up, so, we sometimes, need to view one in the background of other. The Mughals, and for that matter, all the previous Rulers, beginning from those belonging to the Slave Dynasty, who ruled in the thirteenth century, came from outside India but made India their home. It was quite contrary in the case of Britishers who made India a colony. "She had never been drawn into a political and economic system", observed K.S. Shelvankar in his book *The Problem of India* (1940), "whose centre of gravity lay outside her soil, never been subjected to a ruling class which was, and which remained, permanently alien in origin and character."[1] This obsevation gets support from the fact that the Britishers have gone from India (although they have not left India because the legacy of British colonialism still persists) and the part of the people belonging to the ethnic groups of the earlier rulers demanded and got Pakistan and the rest of these continue to *adore* Bharat as their mother-land.

There are no two opinions about this fact that during the period prior to the Rule of Britishers, only the Rulers changed and the economic set-up, by and large, remained intact. But the Britishers brought about a change in the economic set-up followed by the gradual decline of the economic conditions of the people of India. In one word it was a colonial economic set-up. The economic policies of the British Crown, as consequent upon that, adversely affected the rural as well as urban economy of the country, in reducing India into a 'British-Pocket' and thus presenting "a paradox of a poor people living in a rich country."[2] The only beneficiaries during the British *Raj* were the *zamindars* and landlords. "Along with the princes of protected States" writes Bipin Chandra, "that became the cheif political supporters of the foreign rulers and opposed the rising national movement. Realising that they owed their existence to British Rule they tried hard to maintain and perpetuate it."[3] The founders of first Singh Sabha, who hailed from the Sikh aristocracy, belonged to this very category of beneficiaries. The British Government was very keen to win over the Sikhs and this it did while bribing the leaders of the first Singh Sabha namely Baba (Sir) Khem Singh Bedi (1872-1941), Thakur Singh Sandhawalia (1837-1887), Kanwar Bikram Singh of Kapurthala (d. 1887) and others, through granting them pensions and *Jāgīrs*.[4]

How did the first Singh Sabha came into existence ? The four young Sikh boys, namely Aya Singh, Attar Singh, Sadhu

Singh and Santokh Slngh, studying in Church Mission School at Amritsar, when disclosed their intentions for conversion into Christianity (but, were successfully dissuaded) caused sufficient alarm in the Sikh-world. To counteract this tendency of conversion taking shape in the minds of the Sikh youth and to look into the causes responsible for general decline in the Sikh society and to adopt measures for its redemption conscientious among the Sikhs like Sardar Thakur Sing Sandhanwalia, Baba Sir Khem Singh Bedi and Kanwar Bikram Singh of State of Kapurthala, met at Amritsar in 1873 and proposed the formation of the Singh Sabha. The proposal was given a practical shape and the first Singh Sabha was registered under the provision of Act XXI of 1860. Sardar Thakur Singh Sandhanwalia was made its First President and Giani Gian Singh its First Secretary and its first meeting was convened on 1st October, 1873 at the Manji Sahib, in the vicinity of Golden Temple.[5] This meeting was attended by all the sections of the Sikh society. The main objective delineated for the Singh Sabha was to restore the Sikh religion of the Founder-Guru Nanak (and its continuers, the following nine Gurus) culminating in creating Order of *Khālsā*.

The said alarm in the Sikh-world was well-founded as there were couple of other reasons that made the Sikhs alert to combat against their adversaries. Giani Dit Singh, the editor of *Khalsa Akhbar* (Lahore) in his note published in the issue of May, 25, 1894, referring to an English newspaper writers, that,

> ......Just as we do not see any Buddhists in the country except in images, in the same fashion the Sikhs, who are now, here and there, visible in their turbans and their other religious forms like wrist-bangles and swords, will be seen only in pictures in

> museums. Their own sons and grandsons turning Christians and clad in coats and trousers and sporting mushroom like caps will go to see them in the museums and say in their pidgin Panjabi; Look, that is the picture of a Sikh—'the tribe that inhabited this country once upon a time'. (Because) efforts of those who wish to resist the onslaught of Christianity are feeble and will prove abortive.. ...[6]

Again in the issue dated April 22, 1905, the *Khalsa Advocate*, published from Amritsar, pointed out an "Occupant of a *buṅgā* in the precincts of the Taran Taran Gurdwara who had embraced Christianity and hung a Cross on a wall of it turning it thereby into a chapel."[7]

Apart from the above quoted references there were number of other factors highlighting the influence of Christianity that haunted the Sikhs. Maharaja Daleep Singh, in the year 1853 got converted into Christianity and rendered financial assistance for the spreading of newly acquired faith. Funds also flowed from the treasury of Sikh Raja of Kapurthala to be used for propagating the Christian Faith. Also, Kanwar Harnam Singh the nephew of the Raja of Kapurthala embraced Christianity. The norms of the ruling elite are imbibed as models by the common folk. The phenomenon of conversion of the Sikh ruling elite into Christianity, therefore, was against the interest of Sikhism and this trend had to be fought against and eliminated.

An influx af Christian missionaries also spearheaded the cause of Charistian proselytization. John C. Lowrie, the first protestant missionary who came to the Panjab in the year 1834 at the instance of American Presbysterian Church, established a Mission at Ludhiana in the same year during the regime of Maharaja Ranjit Singh (1780-1839). C. W, Forman and John Newton two members of this Mission after rhe fall of Maharaja's empire in 1849 spread out their field of missionrry activities to Lahore the then capital of Panjab.

The Church of England, The Baptist Mission, Cambridge Mission and the Church of Scotland and others also rendered their services in propagating the Christian Faith.

Besides several cases of Individual conversions there are ample evidences to show that the missionaries launched mass movements in different parts of the Northern India. The mass movements helped both the parties, because these minimized the chances for the converts to return to their original faiths. Mostly, the new converts were from the stock of *Cūrās and Camārs*, J. Waskom Pickett's book, *Christian Mass Movements in India* (1933) is full of references of mass conversions. Referring to mass conversions at Sialkot, Pickett writes that five hundred *Cūrās* embraced Christianity.[8]

In the issue of *Khalsa Samacar* dated September 11, 1919, it is reported that thousands of Hindu *Camārs* belonging to thirty seven districts of Meerut were converted into Christian fold and equal number of these were waiting for their turn.

In addition to fighting against the onslaught of Christianity, the Singh Sabha had also to counteract the propaganda of Arya Samaj, the indigenous movement, injurious to the Sikh psyche. Swami Dayanand (1824-1883), who founded Arya Samaj in 1875, in his book *Satyarth Prakash*[9] also published in 1875, made some remarks about Guru Nanak, which hurt the sentiments of the Sikh community. The things changed in due course of time, but these remain confined to some individuals. Ganda Singh, the great Sikh historian setting the record stright writes :

> When Sardar Bhagat Singh of Kanpur brought certain disparaging remarks to the notice of Swami

Dayanand, he according to the statement of Sadhu Surjan Singh (*Aftab-i-Panjab*), December 17, 1888, *Ahwal-i-Arya* p. 91-2 94-5; Kalyan Das, *Sachi-Khoj*, i, 154-5) in reply thereto wrote to him not anly that his views had undergone a change since his visit to the Panjab, but also that he would soon expunge the objectionable passages from *Satyarth Prakash.*[10]

"But Swami Dayanand's first visit to the Panjab" adds Ganda Singh, "where he stayed for about eighteen months (March 1877-August 1878) was to be his last. He could not, therefore, fulfil his promise and delete the passages referred to above."[11]

Prem Lata, in her book *Swami Dayanand Saraswati* (1990), very recently published, while writing under the caption, '*The First Satyarthaprakasha*' has drawn our attention to a very significant fact. She writes, that,

> .....Nevertheless an important and far-reaching decision was finally taken at Benares, and that was the publication of Dayanand's lectures. The idea had originated at Aligarh, where the Swami had a talk about it with Raja Jaikishan Das. Chandra Shekhar, a Maharashtrian Pandit, was appointed translator and the work was taken up in June 1874. At this period, the Swami was busy writing the book. He had a problem with Hindi because he did not know the language well enough, having familiarized himself largely with Sanskrit alone. So in all probability he made the pandit, who helped him with the work, render into Hindi what he dictated or wrote in Sanskrit. He did not take sufficient care to verify if what Chander Shekhar finally wrote was in accordance with what he had intended.[12]

All these facts point to one thing that something some where had gone wrong.

But much more serious thing was the subversion that took place in the sphere of Sikh ethos, that too during the so called Sikh *raj* of Maharaja Ranjit Singh. Whenever and wherever the people adopt the Religion of the Ruler for material or moral gains, such as respectability etc. it inevitably adversely affects the true spirit of that religion for the simple reason that it is not rooted in their Beings and their formal participation only gathers dust on the clean mirror of the concerned religion. This happened in the case of the Sikh religion when patronised by the Maharaja. Many Hindus embraced Sikhism with the result that the *Brāhamṇical* practices, discarded by the Gurus creeped into it and this subverted the true spirit of the Sikh religion. The said subversion fairly reflects from the records[12]* that tell us that the ceremony of *sati* was performed at the death of Maharaja Ranjit Singh. Prior to the formation of the Singh Sabha, the Nirankari Movement founded by Dyal Das (1785-1855), contemporary of Maharaja, in fact was to redeem Sikhism of *brāhamaṇical* practices. The Sikh religion was to be *de-brāhamanised*. The Singh Sabha, took it up as one of the major task, since without accomplishing it the crisis of Sikh identity could not be resolved. Bhai Kahan Singh Nabha (1861-1938) took it up as a mission.

Kahan Singh Nabha made use of his scholarship to propagate the ideals of Singh Sabha. During the course of Arya-Sikh relations a stage came when the protagonists of Arya Samaj, in order to undermine the Sikh identity, started, in a way, a campaign to categorise Sikhism as a sect of Hinduism. To counteract this campaign Bhai Kahan Singh Nabha came forward with his thesis that 'the Sikhs are not Hindus' in his book, *Ham Hindu Nahin* in Hindi, published in

1897. It was made amply clear in the preface that the author had written this book for those, "who not withstanding being a Sikh accept themselves to be the adherents of Hinduism and in following the precepts of *Gurbāṇi* and in considering Sikhism *different* (emphasis is ours) from and higher than Hinduism does not suit them."[13] In other words he wrote this book for Hinduised Sikhs.

The book *Ham Hindu Nahin* is in the form of a dialogue between two characters who are not given any formal name, but are simply mentioned as Hindu and Sikh. The discussion between the two covers as many as fourteen subjects, such as, scriptures, caste-system, re-incarnation, gods and godesses, idoltry and fasting etc. and concludes in disarming Hindu character of his notion that 'the Sikh are Hindus. "The Sikhism *is* different from the Hinduism and other religions and Sikh *Qaum* is like other *Qaums* a distinct one," alright, but in the words of the author, "it does not suggest at all that you [the Sikh] fight against the Hindus and those belonging to other religions and you criticise their religions and do not consider your country men as your brethren, and earn the wrath of your motherland. Rather, you should practise the dictum of your *Satguru* that, 'we are the sons of one Father.'[14]

There is yet one more dimension of Bhai Kahan Singh Nabha's attempt at other than establishing the identity of the Sikhs independent of and distinct from especially, the Hindus. This 'other than' has reference to the author's inclination towards British Masters whom he has eulogized in the book, number of times. At one place, the Sikh (character) tells "even now more than seventy thousand *Khālsā* are rendering military service for the defence of British Government which is beneficial in its mode of functioning."[15] Again Kahan Singh

Nabha was of the view that "it was high time that the Sikhs with the help of *raj* [of Britishers] based on Justice should improve their lot, religious as well as social."[16]

The moral obligation on the part of the Sikhs to be *Namak halāl* enlisted as *rehat* and mentioned in the book[17] has been rightly inferred by Joginder Singh meaning thereby, "loyalty to the British Crown."[18] But, one finds it, rather, difficult to agree with him when he writes that this should not be construed that, "the author [Kahan Singh Nabha] is an apologist of the British *raj*. He is an apologist, but of the Sikh community."[19] Rather, in our opinion Kahan Singh Nabha, under the given set of circumstances, happens to be an apologist, simultaneously, of both the British *raj* and the Sikh community, may be in disguised form.

Our author, Bhai Vir Singh, too was the protagonist of the Singh Sabha, which he joined in 1892 and in the opinion of Balbir Singh, "Bhai Vir Singh's literature is the product of Singh Sabha movement.........."[20]

Now let us turn to Bhai Vir Singh's trilogy. It is a trilogy in which certain sentiment rather than a certain character forms link between the three. And the choice is not arbitrary. It is trilogy, that depicts historical past, we are concerned with. Then, it is a piece of prose-fiction. Our author's choice, too, is most appropriate. The form of prose-fiction is rightly said to be the most effective instrument, if handled properly, in the hands of a missionary, Bhai Sahib never fails as a missionary. He is, rather, *adorned* by his devotees. We are told by his biographers that he studisd and passed his entrance examination from Church Mission School at Amritsar. Part of the credit, for the missionary zeal, he imbibed, certainly goes to this very institution. To add, it was this institute which prevailed upon the Sikh sentiment of four

Sikh students which consequently led to the formation of Singh Sabha.

Bhai Sahib's choicest reader of this trilogy, at least, was no other than women-folk. Again, thischoice was not without merit. Generally speaking, only the women-folk during that period knew Panjabi in Gurmukhi script. The men-folk, if educated, knew English and/or Urdu. The choice of women-folk as a reader, has no doubt, adversely affected the art of fiction, but this is immaterial Bhai Sahib's main concern was not to create art-forms, but to preach effectively, and, which he did. Bhai Sahib was interested in educating the family-unit, the way he desired, that could form the essential base for restructuring contemporary Sikh society. Hence, his focus was on women-folk. He made use of device of plat-form where he could address his women readers and impress upon them to adopt Sundri and Sheel Kaur as models.[21] He does not altogether ignore his men-folk as readers, But, in both the cases his reader is invariably a Sikh, who, falls short of the Sikh ideal and, therefore a fit case for eoaxing.

Bhai Sahib's entire focus, in this trilogy, is three-fold : (i) Hindus are coward (ii) Sikhs are brave and (iii) the Rulers, identified as Turk, are cruel and debauche. In *Sundri* when Balwant Singh a neo-convert to Sikh faith after the abduction of Surasti (later on named Sundri), his sister, brings her back, from the capativity of the Ruler, to the parents, rather than expressing their admiration on his heroic act, he is rebuked, insteaJ, thus :

> What have you done damned fellow ! Will the Turk forgive us now ? The moment he discovers that our son is a Sikh he would doom all of us. And moreover you have snatched away the girl from him he would swallow us all like a starving lion.

> Be a good boy and hand-over the girl to the person from whose captivity you have brought her.[22]

Our author also comments on the general tone of administration as :"............The beautiful women, wealth and pelf could hardly be the possession of a Hindu."[23] The above dialogue and comments, reveal, *fairly well*, Bhai Sahib's grasp of the situation, There is no denying the fact that there were Hindus who were cowards; there were Sikhs who were brave; and there were Rulers who were cruel and debauche. But, to create an impression that all the Hindus were coward; all the Sikhs were brave and all the Rulers were cruel and debauche, this scheme of thought smells a design. The cowardice, the bravery, cruelty and debauchery emerge simultaneously, and the catalytic agent, no doubt, is the Ruler. So, the main focus is on the despicable conduct of the Ruler. This is not an isolated thing. It was a trend enlarged as phenomenon, that reveals its true nature, only, when viewed in its proper historical perspective. Pandit Sunder Lal's observations, while writing on Nawab Vajid Ali Shah, in his book *San Satawan* in this context, are quite revealing. He writes :

> In the word of Sir John this was company's general practice that whenever they took over any State, to denigrte the Raja of that State in the eyes of his subject, they used to cook stories against his character. Unfortunately, books written by people like Arnold based on fictious stories served as a base material for sevral novels. The concocted sin of Vajid Ali Shah were carried on from one book to another and even today, innumerable countrymen of Vajid Ali Shah consider those dirty and false accusation as real.[24]

Out of several attempts aimed at character assissination of Nawab Vajid Ali Shah, one such book is Maulvi Mohammad Najmulghani's *Tarik-e-Awadh* in four volumes. The author, acknowledging the patronage of British Crown, for writing this book of history, expresses his gratitude as follows :

> Though the disinterest of the time has maltreated the Social Sciences and especially history, the time tried its utmost to put off the twinking and burning lamp of history. But the Nature saved it from the unlimited darkness of death and made the British Government as patron of history. Their patronage, protected the lamp of history from stormy winds. It is not required to elaborate and explain the extent of Kingly rewards and honours bestowed upon us every day. Because every intellectual knows it too well.[25]

Maulvi Mohammad Najmulghani, who did play clandestine role of historical dimension, but, after all, was a writer with sensitive soul. He could visulize the contempt of his contemporaries for writing such a book of history. He writes :

> My contemporaries will certaily condemn me on this act that being a Muslim why I wrote a *Kaccā ciṭhā* (misdeeds) of Muslim rulers.[26]

This is nothing but a style of writing of a guilty conscience, whose main purpose was to denigrate the Rulers of the past.

And, according to Sayyid Safdar Hussain,[27] Najmul Ghani was paid rupees ten thousand for the job.

This was the one side of the picture. Let us look at the other side, also. Elliot and Dowson while preparing book on medieval Indian history made selections from the chronicles written by the court writers whose main concern was the Ruler and the battles he fought to expand and to retain his kingdom. These selections were translated and published in eight volumes. These volumes serve as a primary source for those scholars who are not conversent with Persian language. At the moment we are only concerned with the motive of the editors which they expressed right in the Introduction thus :

> ....It will make our native subjects more sensible of the immense advantage accruing to them under the mildness and equity of our rule.[28]

Prof. Khaliq Ahmad Nizami after quoting Elliot's intentions further comments that :

> ...He therefore blackned, 'the Indian past' to glorify the 'British Present' and used medieval Indian history as for the implementation of the formula : 'counterpoise of natives against natives' evolved by the British Army Commission. He was confident that if the "tyranny and capriciousness of despotic rulers of medieval India was discussed in that way it would make the Indians shudder at their past and hail the British regime as a blessing."[29]

Elliot and Dowson's design adds new dimension to our discussion. Thus, to malign the past was part of the plan to glorify the present and the present was British regime.

The plan to glorify the British Rule acquired a peculiar character in the context of Sikh-world. This refers to the prophecies believed to have been made by the Sikh gurus. Max Arthur Macauliffe in the preface to *The Sikh Religion* writes :

> A few of the advantages of the Sikh religion to the

> State may be enumerated. One day as Guru Teg Bahadur was in the top storey of his prison the Emperor Aurangzeb thought he saw him looking towards the South in the direction of the imperial *Zenānā*. He was sent for the next day and charged with this grave breach of oriental etiquette and propriety. The Guru replied, 'Emperor Aurangzeb! I was on the top storey of my prison, but I was not looking in the private apartment or at those queens. I was looking in the direction of the Europeans who are coming from beyond the seas to tear down the *Pardās* and destroy thine empire'.[30]

After that, Macauliffe in the same breath refers to Guru Gobind Singh, who said, that,

> Then shall the English come, and joined by the Khalsa, rule as well in the East as in the West. The Holy Baba Nanak will bestow all wealth on them.[31]

Deriving results from these prophecies, Macauliffe concludes that,

> It is such prophecies as these.........which have made the Sikh among the bravest, the most loyal and devoted subject of the British Crown.[32]

In this way the Sikhs, using Sant Singh Sekhon's expression "were indeed lionised by their conquerors."[33]

Regarding the sources of such prophecies Macauliffe only refers such as "Sikh writers state (p. xviii) or "the following written by one of them', (p. xix). It would be quite futile to search for the authors of these prophecies. These are the creations of the collective unconscious. The masses have been preserving their aspirations in these forms. Any one who collects them at one place does not become their author and also does not remian only a collector. One who collects, also does that motivated by certain needs. The above quoted prophecies, so to say, associated with the Sikh Gurus, depict the aspirations of those alone, for whom the British Rule had proved a blessing. They only wanted to have been sanctioned by the Sikh Gurus.

It is no more surprising, now, at this stage of our investigation to find clauses such as 'loyalty to the Govt,' and disqualifying those who were suspect in the eyes of the Government for becoming members etc.[34] in the Constitution of Singh Sabha. Bhai Sahib was ideologue of Singh Sabha movement which he joined in the year 1892. He was loyal to the British Crown and his loyalty was very much inaccord with the objectives of the Singh Sabha. Any attemt to refute this charge of 'loyalty to the British Crown' must fail. Because, Bhai Sahib himself has provided documentary evidence to that effect. In one of the issues of Khalsa Samacar (weekly) of which he was an editor, under the caption, 'Blessings of the British Regime', he writes :

> It was perpetual anxiety earlier as to how to spend this life, whereas, the question now is how best we are to live it. We are free of any worry from the enemies, facilities e. g. railways, telegraph etc. hospitals and post-offices are there to cater to our needs. Who has brought these blessings ? Soley, because of the grace of the British regime we have all of them. So, we should be beholden to this regime and must prove ourselves to be the loyalist citizen.[35]

Obviously, the benefits enumerated are of material nature.

This 'way of life' continued to be propagated through *Khalsa Samacar*, at least, uptill November 1916—the record we have been able to go through.[36] The reference to Bhai

Vir Singh, in the much talked about secret C. I. D. Memorandum in D. Petrie's *Recent Developments in Sikh Politics* written in 1911, "as a leading figure in the Sikh revival and as disloyal to the core......as a zealous neo-Sikh and thoroughly anti British"[37] needs to be looked into in the background of his avowed loyalty to British Crown, in a dispassionate manner. The report of the government official obout Bhai Sahib is one thing and certainly not a conclusive proof of his having been 'thoroughly anti-British.' Do we find any reference from the pen or activity of Bhai Sahib—a positive evidencc—that justifies the claim of a section of the Sikh society that Bhai Sahib was not pro-British Crown. There is one commission, of course, on the part of Bhai Sahib that proves otherwise. The Massacre of Jallianwala Bagh occured on April 13, 1919 and in Amritsar. Rabindra Nath Tagore (1861-1941) wrote a letter to Lord Chelmsford (r. 1916-21) the Viceory of India and returned the title of Knighthood conferred upon him by the British Government in London, in protest. The letter reads as : "The accounts of insults and sufferings, undergone by our brothers in the Panjab, have trickled through the gagged silence, reaching every corner of India, and the universal agony of indignation roused in the hearts of our people has been ignored by our rulers—possibly congratulating themselves for imparting what they imagine a salutary lesson.

The time has come when badges of honour make our shame glaring in their incongruous context of humiliation, and I, for my part, wish to stand shorn of all special distinction by the side of those of my countrymen who, for their so-called insignificance, are liable to suffer a degradation not fit for human beings."[38]

Not that Bhai Sahib kept mum, as generally believed, he, rather advised Indians to co-operate with the British Masters. In the issue of *Khalsa Samacar* dated April 24, 1919, prior to the Editorial, Government's Report under the Caption *Riots in Lahore and Amritsar* is reproduced. Under the subtitle as 'Second Communique' it is informed on behalf of the Government, that "on April 13, 1919 the provision of Cedesus Meeting Act 1911 was enforced in the districts of Amritsar and Lahore.........It was prohibited to organise any meeting in Amritsar and inspite of that a meeting was held at noon, where about six thousand people were present, As this meeting was illegal, so with the help of Indian army consisting of 29 Gorkha, 54 Sikh and 59 Sindh Rifles, the gathering was scattered with the result many died and were injured. Now there is a calm and quite in the city and the shops are likely to be opened on April 16."[39]

The above quoted Report is followed by the Editorial which has two paragraphs. It is the second paragraph of the Editorial which is relevant to our discussion and therefore, we translate it and place it before you in verbatim, that follows :

> It is now time *Khalsā Ji* to remain alert and vigilant. You have always been supporting the cause of peace. You don't indulge in any *raulā* and help the Government to restore order at every place. Hindu and Muslim brethren ! restore peace in your village, cities and *Muhallas* and while doing so serve the cause of the country and render true service to the government.[40]

Then, in the last few lines of the paragraph, there is reference to the Message of Chief Khalsa Diwan, addressed to the *Sikh Qaum*, and to the similar kind of Messages published by the leaders of Hindu and Muslim communities appealing to the Panjabis to restore law and order.

The Editorial is followed by the Message which in the name of the rich tradition of *Rāj Bhakati* of the *Sikh Qaum* (what a fall from *Gurūbhakti* to *Rājbhakti* !) appeals to them to help the Government and the rulers in restoring law and order in the country. The Message on behalf of the Chief Khalsa Diwan, is signed by Baghel Singh Raj Bahadur (President), Raghbir Singh Sandhawalia Hony. O. B. E. (Vice President) and Sunder Singh Majithia, Additional Member Legislative Council, Government of India, (Hony. Secretary).[41]

Sir Muhammad Iqbal (1877-1938), who was at Lahore during the times of Massacre of Jallianwala Bagh, in one of his letter dated April 20, 1919 and addressed to Khan Niaz Aldin Khan wrote that ;

> ....You must have read from the news paper that Martial Law has been imposed in Lahore. The rules are forced to do so. But, the peace-loving people need not to be scared of.[42]

Muhammad Iqbal decidely falls in the line of Bhai Sahib and both failed in imbibing the spirit of freedom only expected of a great soul like that of Tagore.

Not that we deny the historicity of the sufferings of some of the Sikh Gurus and their followers at the hands of certain Rulers of the past and intend to exonerate them, our only purpose is to expose the trend, at a specific point of time, commissioned by she British Rulers to denigrate their predecessors, to meet their political ends. And, Bhai Sahib, in our estimate, was too willing a partner in this campaign. He was a person with very delicate nature. It is safer also to criticise and condemn those who are no morc alive or no more in power. But, it requires a courage of conviction to denounce those who can make or mar your future. We do not think it is difficult at all to identify the class of writers to which Bhai Sahib belongs to.

Bhai Sahib, as a writer, aimed at restructuring contemporary Sikh society in the pattern, evolved by the Singh Sabha Movement, whose main concern, besides other things, was to remain on the right hand side of the British Masters, It was an attempt and (to the greater extent successful one) once again after Maharaja Ranjit Singh to alienate the contemporary Sikh society from the teaching and the practice of the Sikh Gurus, and its psychology, in quite visible form, continues to subsist even today, although, the Rulers are no other than our own *brethren.*

Bhai Sahib's condemnation of the Rulers of the past, was, in the final analysis, prompted by his motive to glorify the British Rule. This shows that he was not system—conscious and consequently that led him to a paradoxical situation. Had he been system-conscious he would have followed the Path shown by the Sikh Gurus, who had condemned any system built up to perpetuate dark human passions epitiomised as *Māyā.*[43]

Bhai Sahib's admiration for Maharaja Ranjit Singh[44] was very much in tune with the Sikh psyche that was evolved by the Singh Sabha Movement. exalting feudalism, and in the words of Giani Sher Singh :

> Ranjit [Singh] was a king and he tried to make the Sikh religion kingly. The supply of marble, precious stones, gold, large estate and costly canopies, for the Gurdwaras were considered by him to be the means of serving Sikhism.[45]

The sarcasm is quite clear. Again, Bhai Vir Singh in one of his tract entitled *Prarathanā* (The Prayer) published by the Khalsa Tract Society, approvingly mentions Wazir Dhyan Singh addressing the Maharaja as *sacā Pādśāh.*[46]

Contrary to the demands of normal psychical behaviour, Bhai Vir Singh viewed the historical past inconsistent with the attitude he professed towards the contemporary regime. Normally, one's affinity with the past is a direct reflection of one's mode of living in the present. To elaborate : only those persons can be said, mentally and morally well-equipped, to discern the revolutionary contents from their amorphous cultural heritage, who are decidely committed to nothing less than revolution. Bhai Vir Singh defies our hypothesis, and, to his disadvantage. In short, Bhai Sahib was critical about the Rulers of the past, but, he believed in forging comfortable relations with the Brilish Crown. Thus, we find him *involved* in a paradoxical situation—situation, only, apparently absurd, but actually true.

References and Notes

1. Quoted in Jawahar Lal Nehru, *The Discovery of India*, p. 301.
2. Bipin Chandra, *Modern India*, p. 195.
3. *Ibid*. p. 189.
4. G. S Dhillon, *Character and Impact of the Singh Sabha Movement on the History of Panjab*. pp. 50-57. For more details, see : Lepel Griffin, *The Punjab Chiefs*.
5. As regard to the period of the formation of First Singh Sabha there are two opinions. A large number of scholars agree that the date of the formation of First

Singh Sabha was 1st October (Dussehra), 1873. The centenary of Singh Sabha was also observed keeping the year 1873 in view. But scholars like Kahan Singh Nabha, Bhai Vir Singh himself, and Giani Sher Singh, subscribe to the view that the First Singh Sabha was formed in 1872.

see : i. Kahan Singh Nabha, *Mahan Kośa* p. 145

ii. Bhai Vir Singh, *Satwant Kaur* (March 1968) n. p. 243.

iii. Giani Sher Singh, *Philosophy of Sikhism*. p, 6.

6. Quoted in Harbans Singh, "Origins of the Singh Sabha" in *The Singh Sabha and other Socio-Religious Movements in the Panjab* p. 24. Also see : pp. 25-31.
7. *Idem.*
8. *Ibid*. p. 30. Also see Appendix C : 'Baba Naudh Singh—A Story of Conversion'
9. Swami Dayanand, *Satyarath Prakaś* pp. 233-234.

10-11. Ganda Singh, "Bhai Vir Singh and his Times" in Gurbachan Singh Talib, (Ed.) *Bhai Vir Singh, Life Times and Works*, p. 24.

12. Prem Lata, *Swami Dayanand Sarswati* p. 105.

12a. John Martin Honighberger, *Thirty Years in the East.*

13. Kahan Singh Nabha, *Hum Hindu Nahin* pp. 2,3 (The full title is : *Ham Hindu Nahin : Arthat Hindu Musalman Ādi Kom Se Bhin.*)
14. *Ibid* p. 1. (Request from the Author)
15. *Ibid* p. 140
16. *Ibid* p. 152
17. *Ibid* p. 32
18. Joginder Singh, "Bhai Kahan Singh's Ham Hindu Nahin : Polemic or Social Document" in *Journal of Sikh Studies* Vol. XIV, No. 1. February, 19?7. p. 72

19. *Ibid* p. 73
20. Balbir Singh, *Kalam Di Karamat* p. 26.
21. *Sundri* pp. 111-112; *Bijay Singh* pp. 148-149. 155; *Satwant Kaur*, pp. 79, 86.
22. *Sundri* p. 8. Also see, *Bijay Singh* pp. 10-11; *Satwant Kaur* pp. 16, 26.
23. *Sundri* pp. 2-3.
24. Sunder Lal, *San Satawan* p, 27.
25. Maulana Muhammad Najamulghani *Tarikh-e-Awadh*. pp. 3-4.
26. *Ibid* p. 5.
27. Sayyid Safdar Hussain, *Lakhnow Ki Tehzibi-Miras* p. 13.
28. Khaliq Ahmad Nizami and Abdur Rashid "General Criticism of Elliot's Approach to Medieval Indian History" in *Elliot and Dowson History of India* p. 763.
29. *Idem*.
30. M.A. Macauliffe, *The Sikh Religion* vol. 1. p. xviil (Preface).
31. *Ibid* p. xix.
32. *Idem*.
33. Ref. 36 p. 11,
34. i. Shamsher Singh Ashok *Panjab Dian Lehran* p. 181. Clause 5 and 10.
    ii. Jagjit Singh, "Singh Sabha Lehar", in Ganda Singh (Ed.) *Panjab* p. 65.
35. *Khalsa Samacar* January 21, 1901.
36. *Khalsa Samacar* April 29. 1909 p. 5; May 5; 1913, p. 7; October 16, 1916, p. 5; November 20, 1913, p. 4.
37. Ganda Singh, (Ed.) *The Panjab Past and Present* Oct, 1972, Vol. IV, Part II. (Bhai Sahib Volume) p. 107.
38. Edward, J. Thompson, *Rabindra Nath Tagore : His Life and Work*, p. 43.
39. *Khalsa Samacar* pp. 1-2.

40. *Ibid* p. 2.

We have attributed the Editorial to Bhai Vir Singh and some people are very likely to dispute this statement of fact. To set the record straight we quote the relevant part from the statement of Giani Mahan Singh specifically clarifying the issue of Editor of *Khalsa Samacar*. "When the paper started in 1899" writes Giani Mahan Singh "it was not at all obligatory to mention the name of Editor. This is why inspite of the fact that for number of years the paper was edited by Bhai Sahib, his name never appeared as a Editor. Uptill 1914 many persons such as Bhai Sant Ram, Bhai Sohan Singh and Baba Ganga Singh Bedi etc. joined as Editor or as sub-editor but Bhai Sahib continued to be the Chief-Editor. Sometimes in 1914 Bhai Sewa Singh joined as sub-editor and continued to serve under the supervision of Bhai Sahib till 1945"—Giani Mahan Singh *Khalsa Samacar* (1950) pp. 85-86. Therefore, we have every reason to attribute the said Editorial to Bhai Sahib.

41. *Idem*.

42. *Makatib-e-Iqbal*, p. 26

43. i. As a King (not only) one rules over the others.
But, also exploits others and amasses riches. (Māyā)
—*Adi Granth* pp. 391-392

ii. The King, worthy of throne should occupy it
Only those kings are true kings
who have realized the Truth.
The kings (that we have) are not true one.
For they are torn by duality that leads to suffering.
—*Adi Granth* p. 1088.

44. *Sundri* p. 72.

45. Sher Singh, *The Philosophy of Sikhism* p. 13

46. Quoted in Balbir Singh. *Lammi Nadar* p. 61.

CONCLUSION

The Sikh psyche, taking shape in the hands of Guru Nanak, was at once rebellious against the State and the *Brāhmaṇical* order and Compassionate, in its contents. The continuers of the Sikh tradition, upto Guru Arjan, only added certain measures, at every step, to build up the *Saṅgat* outside caste-structure, with identity of its own. The State and the Sikh Gurus, however, always remained vigilant about each other's activities. Guru Arjan had become a force to reckon with The Mughal monarchy could not and did not tolerate it and this led to the martyrdom of Guru Arjan. The Sikh movement, not at all deviating from its course, took a new turn. Guru Hargobind, the Sixth Guru, initiated a process of building up a State, egalitarian in character, within the Empire. The State and the Sikh Gurus, as usual, continued to interfere with each other's affairs. An inevitable result was the second martyrdom, the martyrdom of Guru Tegh Bahadur. Guru Gobind Singh, the Tenth Guru, created *Khālsā* to build up an armed revolt against the State. The *Khālsā* under the leadership of the Guru fought against the State. The State did not 'wither away' and the *Khālsā*, suffered a crushing defeat. The Guru enjoined Banda Singh Bahadur with 'holy mission' who successfully fought against the State establised an egalitarian State in Sirhand, but, that was just for a while. After the persecution of Banda Singh Bahadur in Delhi, followed by the policies of the State aimed at eliminating the Sikhs as a community, forced the Sikhs to retire to mountains and forests. The Sikhs kept up their rebellious spirit engaged in guerilla warfare against the State. It is this phase of the Sikh history that forms the subject-matter of the trilogy. This phase is followed by an era of the Sikh *misals* The Sikh movement, in the hands of *misaldārs*, switched over to feudalism and the character of the movement was subverted which reached at its zenith during the 'Sikh Raj' of Maharaja Ranjit Singh.

Maharaja Ranjit Singh's Empire was annexed into British Empire. When Bhai Vir Singh wrote and published the trilogy the Britishers had already established themselves as an Empire. The Singh Sabha Movement came up in order to preserve the glorious heritage of the Sikhs and to propagate the same to the contemporary Sikh Society. In this venture the Singh Sabha sought the *help* of the British Masters against avowed loyalty to the British Crown. The Singh Sabha managed the patronage of the British Masters and partly used it in the interest of Sikhism when through *Pāṭh* (recitation of *Gurbāṇi*), *Kirtan* (Singing of *Gurbāṇi*) and the observance of number of ceremonies e.g. *Kirya* (death ceremony), *Anand Kāraj* (marriage ceremony) etc. the Sabha *helped* the Sikhs to remain wedded to *Adi Grantha*, the Living Guru. Had it not happened, some may suggest, it would not have been possible, today, to evaluate the role of the Singh Sabha, in the absence of long bearded Sikhs with turbans on their heads But, this act on the part of the Singh Sabha—seeking patronage—did result in diluting the character of the Sikh tradition, revolutionary in its contents. Bhai Vir Singh was a willing partner and, therefore, guilty of subverting an anti-coercive-State character of the Sikh movement nourished by the blood of the Sikh Gurus and their followers in order to first establish an egalitarian society followed by a State egalitarian in character.

APPENDIX A

A REVIEW OF SOURCES

For writing trilogy Bhai Vir Singh manipulated material derived from various sources, such as, folk song, oral tradition, *Gurbāṇi*, Sikh Chronicles, History, travelogue and archaeological evidences etc.

Sundri is based on Panjabi folk song which is given in the Appendix I of the text. The writer of this appendix, Sardar Mahan Singh tells that "it [*Sundri*] is based on a song which was published at that time also," (i. e. at the time of publication (of the first edition of *Sundri*). This is an old song which old ladies in olden times used to sing."[1] Later, he adds more to it. "*Sundri* was not yet printed" tells Sardar Mahan Singh, "When Bhai Sahib Takhat Singh got the manuscript from the author [Bhai Vir Singh] and read it to Vakil Sardar Chand Singh of Ferozpur. One maid-servant at the latter's residence abruptly remarked that Sardarji, the story that you are reading reminds me of a song. Then, she sang that very song which is given in the preceding pages."[2]

The said song was in vogue during the period when *Sundri* was written. This means, that the episode of Sundri had already become part of folk-lore and an integral part of the Sikh psyche.

The oral tradition, as regard to the details, too was availed of while giving shape to *Sundri*.

The Sikh Chronicles like *Ratan Sinah Bhangu's* (d. 1846) *Pracin Paṅth Prakaś* (1841) and *Tawarikh Guru Khalsa* (in

3 volumes) of Giani Gian Singh published in 1892, form major sources for writing *Sundri.* Captain Murray, under the inspiration of Sir David Ochterlony, wrote down an account of *Khalsa Panth* in 1809 at Ludhiana, as told by Ratan Singh. This very account, later on, Ratan Singh himself wrote and published in 1841 in the form of verse.[3] This book covers the period of Sikh history right from the times of the Gurus concluding with third quarter of the eighteenth century. *Tawarikh Guru Khalsa* commences its journey from the times of Guru Nanak, while discussing about twelve *msals*, ends with the reign of successors of Maharaja Ranjit Singh.

The historical sources are not altogether left out. The "description of thick forests in *Sundri*" (2nd chapter) according to the information of Kirpal Singh, based on Sir Jadu Nath Sarkar's monumental work, *The Fall of Mughal Empire*, "literally tallies with the description given by Sujan Rai Bhandari in 1676 in his book the *Khulsat-ut.Twārikh.*[4] The source, however, has not been disclosed by the author. Again, "the account of the persecution of the Sikhs as given in the opening paragraphs of the 12th chapter of *Sundri*," reveals Kirpal Singh, "is identical with the description given by Hari Ram Gupta in his *History of the Sikhs.*"[5] This 'identical description' does not cast any reflection on Bhai Vir Singh. Firstly, Hari Ram Gupta's *History of Sikhs* (1937) is much later a publication than *Sundrī*. Secondly, the novelist and the historian, both have taken material from *Pracin Panth Prakaś.*[6]

We also find footnoes in case of *Sundri*. These footnotes refer to historical material derived from the books on History, such as, Karam Singh's *Banda Bahadur*, *Jang-nama* by Qazi Noor Muhammad; Muhammad Latif's *History of Panjab*, *Farah-tu-Nazreen* by Mohammad Aslim, *Umdat-ut-Twarikh* of

Sohan Lal Suri, Malcolm's *Sketch of the Sikhs*, *Transformation of Sikhism* by Gokul Chand Narang and host of others. These footnotes as stated by Sardar Mahan Singh[7] and later pointed out by Surinder Singh Narula in his book *Bhai Vir Singh*[8] (n. d.) were later additions incorporated by the author himself as these footnotes are sonspicuously missing from earlier editions. Moreover a good number of these books were published at a much later stages.

In Appendix 2[9] of *Sundri* it is also revealed that Akali Kaur Singh Nihang in his paper *Kashmir Singh Samacar* of January 1936 at page 3 published the photograph of one Major Waryam Singh of Satwara Cantt (Jammu) along with some biograghical details. Major Waryam Singh, in fact, belonged to Village Khanaura, District Hoshirpur. During the times of Guru Dashmesh Patshah (Guru Gobind Singh) one member of his family got himself baptized alongwith Guru Khālsā. This newly baptized Sikh was no other than Sardar Balwant Singh of *Sundri*.

We also find an archaeological evidence in connection with *Sundri*. There is one well in Kahnwana, District Gurdaspur constructed by *Khālsā* in commemoration of Surdri. Gurdwara is also being constructed over there.[10]

The above two references are, of course, later discoveries, but these certainly show two tnings : one, Sundri's heritage and two, that she had already become a respectable and a model to be followed by the Sikhs, especially, by Sikh women.

Bijay Singh, as stated by the author in the Preface to the first edition, is based on both the *Panth Prakaś* and *Twarikh Guru Khalsa*.[11] The two *Panth Prakaś* are : i by Ratan Singh

Bhangu and ii. written by Giani Gian Singh. Gian Singh's *Paṅth Prakaś* is only little elaborated version of Ratan Singh's *Paṅth Prakaś*, which he composed in 1867 and published in 1880. Besides these Sikh Chronicles, the author has also acknowledged having made use of historical writings of, say, Cunningham, Muhammad Latif, M' Gregor and of others.[12] But, when we read the later editions of *Bijay Singh* we find references to certain books in the form of footnotes which are certainly later publications. For instance, Sir Lepel Griffin's books *Ranjit Singh* was first time published in 1905; Gokul Chand Narang's *Transformation of Sikhism* in 1912. This only means that these footnotes are later additions.

The author also derived informations from oral tradition and folk songs.[13]

Satwant Kaur commences its journey straightway without any Preface by the author. Therefore, there is no direct reference at all abobt the sources. But we find plenty of footnotes which tell about various sources, including Sikh Chronicles and books on History. These foot-notes seem to be incorporated at later stages.

Sundri, *Bijay Singh* and *Satwant Kaur*, all the three heavily derived (or pretend to, while incorporating foot-notes at later stages) material from historical sources, alright, but these by any standard can not be adjudged as books on History. Nor, they succeed in projecting a clean image of Novels (Historical novels or Romances). These are, in fact, of the nature of collage as they also include religion and what not. These can be at the best identified as fictional writings dealing with mid-eighteenth century Sikh history of the Panjab of pre-Partition days of India.

References and Notes

1. *Sundri* (32nd Edition 1966) p. 130
2. *Ibid* p 136
3. Kahan Singh Nabha, *Gursabad Ratnakar*, *Mahan Kośā* p. 594.
4. Sir Jadu Nath Sarkar, *The Fall of Mughal Empire* Vol, I, p. 115. Quoted by Kirpal Singh, "Historical Significance of Sundri, Bijay Singh and Satwant Kaur" in *Bhai Vir Singh* Edited by Ganda Singh p. 81.
5. Kirpal Singh *loc. cit.*
6. *Ibid.* p. 82.
7. *Sundri* p. 136.
8. Surinder Singh Narula, *Bhai Vir Singh* p. 17.
9. *Sundrī* p. 149.
10. *Idem*

11-13. *Bijay Singh* (22nd edition 1967) p. Sassā (Preface).

APPENDIX B

THE DIVINE RIGHT OF KINGSHIP

'The World is divinely ordained', this belief, in medieval times, both in the East and West had provided mutual ideological aid to monarchy and monotheism. As a result it was quite natural to show reverence to a king endowed with divine qualities. This reverence for sovereign, in a due course of time, assumed the form of 'right', later on, was formulated as a theory of 'Divine Right of Kingship.' Thc manifestations of divine qualities in a king, as contemplated in the said theory, can be analysed in the background of functional autonomy of a king. And, we suggest the following course :

1. *King : An Incarnation af God* : 'King is a divine incarnate' this belief was prevalent in Hellenic age in Greece and Rome during pre-Christian era.[1] Alexender the Great (356-325 B. C.) during his life-period was hailed as an incarnate of God and Roman kings were accorded the same kind of respectability after their deaths. Later on, in Christianity the Divinity was transfered and conferred upon Pope, who was under obligation to transfer the same to a king at the time of coronation. When the Reformation (16th cent.) launched an attack on the supremacy of Pope, it indirectly strengthened the notion of 'Divine Right of kingship.'[2]

In India, we find evidence of upholding the theory of 'Divine Right of Kingship' in *Manusmriti*', *Vishnupurana* and *Bhagvata-purana*. Manu is of the view that the Ruler is an incaranation of Great Power, and is an embodiment of eight divine powers.[3] *Visnu-purana* and *Bhagvata-purana* advocate the theory that number of divine powers dwell in the person of king.[4] It was under this pretext that the king was deified as a divine incarnate. There is no specific reference to this kind of theory in Vedic-age and probably it came in to fashion during Brahamanic period.[5]

In Islam too, the king is believed to be a 'Shadow of God'. This notion, in Islam, got into when Arabs captured Persia Iranian interpreted the teachings of Prophet Muhammad in the background of their indigenous culture which had an impact of Indian culture. Especially, the theory, of incarnation, so dear to Indian people had become an integral part of the Iranian psyche. Under this influence the king was hailed as an human-counterpart of 'Great Force'.[6] An accep-tence of person as an Incarnation of God was not in accordance with the Islamic tanets. This problem was resolved by associating divinity with the functioning rather than with the person of a king.[7] The king was addressed as a *Zill-e-Illahi*[8], or 'Shadow of God' and with such other titles.[9]

2. *Functional Similarity* : There exists a functional similarity between God and King. We find references to this effect in West, also[10]. All the (Muslim) kings adhered to this view, as discussed earlier. Taimur (r. 1370-1405) also upheld the same view. He considered the world as a replica of the 'World of Divine', and was of firm conviction that as God is one and has no equal, similarly, there should be one and only one sovereign in the world.[11] Indian thinkers did not lag behind and their views fairly reflect in *Smritis* and *puranas* wherein the functional similarity between divine forces and sovereign is emphasised, time and again.[12] It needs to be pointed out that only righteous kings were accorded this high honour and morally corrupt rulers were looked down upon and also vehemently condemned.[13]

3. *Divine Right of King* ; The view that sanctions divine right to kings neither has its roots in the theory of incarnation nor in the functional similarily between God and kings; it seeks its support from inheritence, which, in a way, is a divine blessing. Sir Albert Filme, the Western thinker was the protagonist of this theory. He was of the view that whatever one gets is one's divine right. Kingship is also a gift of Nature, hence, it amounts to divine right.[14] This way divine right was bracketed with one's birth-right. In the West, James the First had traced his ancestary right from the conquests of his fore-father, William the First.[15] In his view the king was not at all answerable to his subject. The subject who came to the king for justice can not sit as a judge over the actions of their king.[16] These views of James the First, no doubt, were fully supported, but, at the same time, it was also held that any king, whosoever he may be, when acts against the interest of his subject forefeits the right of king as a representative of God on earth. His subject is not under any moral obligation to follow the commands of such a fallen king.[17]

We do not find any reference, categorical in nature, in Hindu scriptures, supporting the 'Divine Right of kings' for the simple reason that this theory was universally accepted and there was hardly any need to put in black and white. According to *Ramayan* and *Mahabharat* the right to succeed the sovereign was reserved only for the *Rajkumar* or prince.

Mughal monarchs came to India while well-armed with the theory of 'Divine Right of Kings'. Abu Sayyid Mirza the grand-father of Babar (r. 1526-1530) the Mughal Emperor, had issued instructions to Yunus Khan the Mughal ruler, that King's commands must be issued under the seal of Mughal dynasty.[18] Babar,[19] also followed the same philosophy and it was put into practice during the Mughal rule in India.

As the 'Divine Right of Kings' was an accepted political norm among the Hindus, this helped the Mughals to use this as a weapon without any resistance from any quarter.

In fact, the purpose *to bestow* divine qualities in the Rulers was to add in to their glory besides moral strength.[20] *Ulemas* deified the commands of the Sultan (*or Pātśāh*) as the orders of *Allāh* and obedience to his commands was, therefore deemed to be a moral duty for one and all. This is why in the Holy verses of Guru Nanak, God is compared to *Sultan* or (*Pātśah*).

References and Notes

1. (i) *Encyclopaedia of Social Sciences*, Entry on 'Divine Right of Kings' vol. V. p. 176.

   (ii) For similar references in various parts of the world also see : A.M. Hocart, *Kingship* Chapter I 'The Divinity of Kings' pp. 1-11.
2. A. S. Altekar, *State and Government in Ancient India* pp- 92-93.
3. (i) Ibid pp. 90-91, Manu VII. 5. 4.

   (ii) A.M. Hocart *op. cit.* p. 89.
4. A. S. Altekar op. cit p. 91.
5. (i) A.M. Hocart *op. cit.* p. 3.

   (ii) A. S. Altekar *op. cit.* p. 89.
6. (i) Muhammad Habib, *Sultan Mahmud of Ghazni.* p. 5.

   (ii) H.G. Rawlinson, *Five Great Monacchies* vol. III p. 202. Quoted in K.M. Ashraf, *Life and Condition of the People of Hindustan* p. 31.

   (iii) K.M. Ashraf *op. cit.* p. 29.

7. *Ibid* p. 31 :

"......This difficulty was solved by associating the virtue of divinity with the office of the *Sultanate* rather than with the person of the *Sultan*. He was designated as *Zill-ullah*, the Shadow of Divine Being. However, did not stop Divine honours from being paid to a *Sultan* or a monarch from ruling over people as 'a God in human from."

8. E. Denison Ross, Sir (Ed) *Fakhir-ul-Din's Tarikh-e-Mubarik Shahi*. Quoted in K.M. Ashraf. *op. cit.* p. 31.

9. Anil Chander Banerjee 'The Islamic kingship in India' *in Indian Historical Quarterly* vol. XIII 1937 No 2.

10. Kern Fritz, *Kingship aud Law in the Middle Ages* (translated with introduction by S.B. Chrimes) pp. 7-8 :

"....Government was conceived of as the image in miniature or the Divine Government of the World." p. 7.

"...And this Divine aspect of Government was deemed to be most satisfactority manifested when one single person ruled as God's Vicar." p. 8.

11. *Mal Būzāt-e-Timuri* (autobiography of Timur) Quoted in R.P. Tripathi, *Some Aspects of Muslim Administration* p. 107 :

"The central point in Timur's conception of sovereignty was his belief that the various offices in an earthly empire are symbols of these in the empire of God............Timur believed that 'Since God is one and hath no partner, therefore, the vice-regent (king) over the land of Lord must be one."

12. A.S. Altekar, *op. cii.* p. 91.

13. *Ibid* pp. 92-93.

14. (i) Sir Robert Filmer, Quoted in J. Neville Figgis *The Theory of the Divine Right of King* p. 153 :

    "Filmer's theory of Divine Right was expressed in a syllogism :

    What is nature to a man exists by Divine Right. Kingship is natural to man, therefore Kingship exists by Divine Right."

    (ii) *Encyclopaedia of Social Sciences* vol 5 p. 176.

15. *Idem.*

16. Kern Fritz. *op. cit.* p. 11.

17. *Ibid* p. 136 :

    "Consequently, it is cometent to decide when a prince because of his unjust deeds, has ceased to be God's deputy and, therefore, has ceased to be a person vested with authority on earth. State deprives the tyrant of the mandate which belongs only to the just kings. The spiritual quality frees the people from the right to obey him."

18. *Tarikh-e-Rashidi* (translated by Elias and Ross p. 172) Quoted in R.P. Tripathi *op. cit.* p. 109.

19. (i) A.S. Beveridges (trs) *Memoirs of Babar* (translation of (*Tuzk-e-Babri*) Vol. I p. 274.

    (ii) *Tarikh-e-Rashidi* translated by Elias and Ross p. 389). Quoted in R.P. Tripathi *op. cit.* p. 111.

20. Ibn Hasan, *The Central Structure of the Mugal Empire* p, 59 :

"The political writers and Jurists were not content with merely emphasising the importance of the office, but forced by the conditions under which they were living, they deliberately introduced into it the divine element to strengthen the principle of authority, and this obedience to the king was made religious duty."

21. Edward Thomas, *The Chronicles of the Pathan Kings of Delhi* pp. 245-250 :

"……The Ulema subscribed to the proposition :

"He who obeys the Sultan, obeys the Lord Merciful."

APPENDIX C

BABA NAUDH SINGH : A STORY OF CONVERSION

The novel depicts rural Panjab, under British Rule, when the main concern of the protagonists of different religious communities was none other than to convert others into their respective cults. Proselytization was not being practised; it was conversion prompted by different motives. Bhai Vir Singh creates a character of a widow whose ardent desire is to meet her dead husband in heaven. She is made to pass through different religious channels before she is conveated into Sikhism, by the grace of ideal Sikh like Baba Naudh Singh, and consequent upon that her desire is 'fulfilled'. The different religious channels made available to Jamuna, (born in Jain family) a Hindu widow, prior to entering into Sikh-fold. are, somehow, coloured. This tendenciousness is a direct reflection of the communal surroundings our author had lived in and fallen victim to the 'climate of opinion'.

Subhag Ji Da Sudhar Hathin Baba Naudh Singh, generally referred to in abridged form as *Baba Naudh Singh* (serialized in the form of tracts since 1907) was first time published in the form of book in the year 1921. By the time, Bhai Sahib had already published, besides the trilogy, *Rana Śurat Singh* (serialized in 1905 and published in incomplete form in 1919) and Raja Lakhdata Singh (1910) to mention only a few. He had, by that time, established Khalsa Tract Society (1894) in collaboration with Bhai Kaur Singh Dhupia and had launched two tracts namely *Nirguṇiara* (1894) and *Khalsa Samacar* (1899). All these activities aimed at propagating Sikh religion. Individual and mass conversions to Sikhism were welcome news to the Sikhs, as well. In one of the issues of *Khalsa Samachar*[1] dated March 20, 1919, conversion of one hundred men of *Boriā Qaum* belonging to Mughalpura (Lahore) and managed by Chief Khalsa Diwan, was hailed and it was expected that two thousand more were likely to join the Sikh-fold. It is in this background that conversion of Jamuna, a widow, into Sikh Faith, needs to be examined.

The story of conversion is very simple. Jamuna was married to a person living at Mandawi, a town in Kathiawar. She was quite young when her husband, aged 25, passed away. In this state of utter helplessness Jamuna was introduced by an old woman to a certain *Tāntrik*. Both the *Tāntrik* and Jamuna moved from Mandawi to Jammu for the aforesaid purpose. He duped her while promising her a meeting with her husband in the heaven, and thus, robbed her of whatever wealth she had. Then, a Christian missionary comes in the life of Jamuna. Jamuna is baptized into Christianity and given the name, Miss Domeli. Now, the Christians, converted from the stock of *cūrās* and *camāras* contemptiously called *Karānis*, tried to woo her for marriage. Here the reference to these Christians as *Kāle kāle, koi Cūriyon Koi Camīarion*[2] by the author is notable. Bhai Sahib's contempt for *cūrās* and *Camiārs* is sufficient evidenee of his psyche being plagued with caste prejudice.

Jamuna, now Miss Domeli, escaped from the net of Christian missionaries and reached Lahore. Here, in the mosque Jamuna was converted into Islam and named Ghulam Fatma by the *Maulvis*. At Lahore, Jamuna, comes across

Ganga Bai, her old acquaintance from Mandawi, who brings her to Bhai Gursharan Singh and his wife Upkar Kaur. Ganga Bai, in the company of this Sikh couple, had earned spiritual wealth and wanted Jamuna to get rid of her miseries born out of attachment to worldly things. Jamuna is impressed by Upkar Kaur but she is reluctant to accept her as guide because of her past bitter experiences. She decided to commit suicide and jumped into the river Ravi. Baba Naudh Singh was reciting *Sukhmahi Sahib* on the river bank when he saw a body floating in the river. He saved her, consoled her, and gave her the name of Subhag.

Subhag undcr the instructions of Baba Naudh Singh developed into a realized soul.

Apart from the attempts made for individual conversions there are references in the novel that show how the preachers of different religious communities were pursuing the course of mass conversions. A certain Arya Samajist visited the village of Baba Naudh Singh and started talking about Guru Nanak in derogatory language. The people got annoyed and rushed towards him with sticks in their hands. He was surrounded by the village-folks when Baba Naudh Singh arrived at. Baba enquired from him that 'What brought the man of clean clothes amidst the folk-people of dirty clothes," ? He replied :

"I have come to convert you all as Arya."[3]

Again,

"We have to convert whole country as Arya."[4]

Baba told him that he had been to Lahore for some months and witnessed all the *tamāśās* or gimmicks. Better if they were left to live the way they liked.

The Arya did not budge and reiteraned his stand. Then, Baba told him that they were better as illiterate and wanted him to share his wisdom, if he had, which transforms the human beings into higher order. The Arya abruptly commented in Hindi that,

"Your Guru too was illiterate this is why you say so."[5]

The entire episode reflects the tone of *Satyārth Prākāś*,[6] wherein Guru Nanak was adjudged by Swaml Dnyanand as unlettered, combined with the injury caused to the Sikh-psyche.

Saifdin, a muslim preacher from Aligarh also arrived at the village and approached the Muslim population that consisted of two families of *zamindārs*, some were weavers others cobblers and washermen. He poisoned the minds of these simple folk and told them that how, in olden times, the Mughals butchered and killed the Hindus and it was in conformity with Islam.[7]

A Christian missionary in order to influence the villagers used to visit and sing songs in praise of Jesus Christ, on harmonium. Frequently, to undermine the sanctity of Ram and Krishan, he used to point out 'black spots' in their lives. One day in the presence of Rajha, a Muslim *Zamindar*, which the latter could not tolerate and in turn pointed out certain bad points in Jesus.[8] The missionary got Ranjha arrested. When Baba Naudh Singh approached the Christian priest, asking for forgiving Ranjha, during this meeting the priest remarked that he thought that Baba had gone to him for conversion into Christianity.[9]

A zealous member of Brahma Samaj, founded by Raja Ram Mohan Rai (b. 1872) at Calcutta, in 1830, also tried to convert people into his religious beliefs but failed and in turn, under the influence of Baba Naudh Singh got (nearly) converted into Sikhism. One Barrister, Madho Das and his wife also developed inclination towards Sikhism.

Arya Samajist, Christian missionary, Muslim and Brahmo Samaj preachers, all failed in the mission to convert people into their respective religious cults in view of the influence of Baba Naudh Singh. Some of them, instead, either got (nearly) converted to Sikhism or were detered.

The under current idea in the novel *is* to convert people into Sikhism. Conversion to Sikhism, engineered by Chief Khalsa Diwan, aimed at providing wider base of support to British Masters. The loyalty to British Crown fairly well echoes in this novel.[10]

References :

1. p. 2
2. *Baba Naudh Singh* (Edition : September, 1985) p. 7
3. *Ibid* p. 24
4. *Ibid* p. 25
5. *Ibid* p. 26
6. Chapter 6 The Rise of British Empire pp. 102-103.
7. *Baba Naudh Sihgh* p. 29
8. *Ibid* p. 35
9. *Ibid* p. 40.
10. *Ibid* pp. 32, 45

WORKS OF BHAI VIR SINGH

(Poetry, Drama, Prose and Fiction)

1898 *Sundri* (Novel) KSA. 32nd Edition : September, 1968

1899-1900 *Bijay Singh* (Novel) KSA. 22nd Edition : September, 1967

1900 *Satwant Kaur* Part I (Novel) KSA. March, 1968

1905 *Rana Surat Singh* (Mahākāvya) KSA.

1907 *Baba Naudh Singh* (Novel) KSA. September, 1965

1910 *Rājā Lakhnātā Singh* (Drama) WHPA.

1921 *Tarel Tupke* (Poetry) WHPA.

1921 *Jiwan Ki Hai* (Poetry) WHPA.

1921 *Lehran Da Haar* (Poetry) KSA.

1922 *Godavari Da Geet* (Poetry) WHPA

1922 *Matak Hulare* (Poetry) KSA.

1922 Bismal More (Poetry) WHPA.

1922 *Bulbul Te Rāhi* (Poetry) WHPA.

1925 *Sri Kalghi Dhar Camatkār* (Biography) KSA.

1927 *Satwant Kaur*, Part II, (Novel) KSA March, 1968

1927 *Bijlian De Haar* (Poetry) KSA.

1928 *Sri Guru Nanak Camatkār* (Biography) KSA.

1929 *Preet Viṇa* (Poetry) KSA

1933 *Kambadi Kalai* (Poetry) KSA.

1938 *Sant Gatha*, Part I, (Prose) KSA.

1948 *Lehar Hulare* (Poetry, Selection) KSA,

1950 *Kant Mheli* (Poetry) KSA.

1951 *Nināna Bharjai* (Poetry, written in 1900) KSA.

1952 *Sri Aṣṭa Guru Camatkar* Part I, (Biography) KSA.

1953 *Mere Saniya Jio* (Poetry) KSA.

1955 *Balam Sākhiyan* (of Guru Nanak and Guru Gobind Singh) KSA.

1956 *Sarva Priya Sikh Dharma* (Prose) KSA.

1968 *Sri Asta Guru Camatkār*, Part II, (Biography) KSA.

1973 *Sahitak Kaliyan* (Poetry) KSA.

1973 *Sikkān Sadhrān* (Poetry) KSA.

1974 *Awaz Ai* (Poetry), Edited by Balbir Singh, KSA.

1974 *Sri Sant Bimlā Singh* (Biography) KSA.

1980 *Pyar Athru* (Poetry) Bhai Vir Singh Sahitya Sadan, New Delhi.

i. KSA : *Khalsa Samacar*, Amritsar.

ii. WHPA : Wazir Hind Press, Amritsar.

BIBLIOGRAPHY A

(Historical Sources)

Ahmad Shah Batalīa, *Tawārikh-i-Hind* (MSS 1818) Language Department, Patiala.

Ali-ud-Dīn Mufti, *Ibrat Nama* (MSS 1854) Panjabi Adabi Academy, Lahore, 1961 (2 vols)

Bhai Chaupa Singh and others, *Rahit Name* Pratap Singh and Sunder Singh, Amritsar.

Bhai Karam Singh, *Maharaja Ala Singh* Khalsa Dewan Prachārak Vidyalya, Taran Taran, 1918.

————*Baba Banda Bahadur* Chief Khālsā Dewan, Amritsar.

Bhāi Santokh Singh, *Sri Guru Pratap Suraj Granth* Caxton Printing Press Lahore, Khalsa Samachar Amritsar. 1929-37 (14 vols).

Elphinstone, *Histary of India, Hindu and Muhammadan Periods.* John Murray, London, 1874.

Ganda Singh, *History of the Gurdwara Shahidganj Lahore, from Its Origin to November* 1935, published by the author, December 1935.

……………………(Tr. Ed.) *Qazi Nur Muhammad's Jang-Nama.* Khalsa College Amritsar, 1939.

G. B. Malleson *Decisive Battles of India from* 1746 *to* 1849 *Inclusive* Reeves and Turner, London, 1888.

Ghūlam Ali Khān, *Siyarul-Imad-us-Saadat* Nawal Kishore, Cawnpore, 1864.

Ghulam Hussain Khan, *Siyatul-Mutakherin* Calcutta. 1836.

Gianī Gian Singh, *Panth Prakaś* Khalsa Tract Society, Amritsar; Murtazai Press, Delhi, 1880.

....*Twārikh Guru Khalsa*, Khalsa Tract Society, Amritsar.

Gokul Chand Nārang *Transformation of the Sikhs or How the Sikhs Became a Political Power* Tribune Press, Lahore, 1912.

H. A. Giles *The Travels of Fa-hien* Cambridge, 1923.

Henry M. Elliot, *History of India As Told By Its Historians* Turbner and Co. London (1967-77) (8 vols)

James Browne, *History of the Origin and Progress of the Sikhs* (India Tracts) The East India Coy, at the Logographic Press, London, 1788.

Joseph Davy Cunningham, *A Histoty of the Sikhs From the Origin of the Nation to the Battles of Sutlej.* John Murray, London. 1949.

Kanhaya Lāl, Rai Bahadur *Tarikh-i-Panjab* Victoria Press, Lahore. 1881.

Lepil. H. Griffin *Ranjit Singh* (Rulers of India Series) Clarendon Press, Oxford 1905.

Le-Pere J. Tieffenthaler, *Descriptton Historique et Geographique De l' Inde.* London. 1788.

Lewis Smith *A Sketch of the Rise, Progress and Termination of the Regular Corps Formed and Commanded by Europeans in the Services of the Native Princer of India, with details of Principal Events and Actions of the Late Marhatta War* Harkarn Press, Calcutta. 1805

Malcolm, Lt. Col. *Sketch of the Sikhs : A Singular*

Nation who Inhabit the Provinces of Punjab John Murry, London. 1817.

Muhammad Latif *History of the Punjab* Central Press Ltd. Calcutta. 1891.

Muhammad Aslam Bin Muhammad Hafiz, *Farhat-un-Nazrin* MSS 1770-71 Archieves Department of the Government of Panjab, Patiala.

Ratan Singh Bhangu *Prāchīn Panth Prakāś* Wazir-i-Hind Press, Amritsar.

Sohan Lal Suri *Umdat-Ut-Twarīkh* Lahore. 1819 (5 vols).

Sukha Singh *Gurbilās Pātashāhi Dasvīn* Sikh Reference Library, Amritsar.

W. H. Mcleod (Tr. Ed.) *The Chaupa Singh Rahit Nāmā* University of Otago Press Dunedin (Newzeland). 1987.

Zaka-Ullah Dehlvi. *Tārīkh-i-Hindustan* Murtazvi Press, Delhi. 1915-17; Aligarh Institute Press. Aligarh. 1919.

BIBLIOGRAPHY - B

Aijaz Hussain, *Adabi Rujhanat* Kitabistan Allahabad, Fifth Edition : May, 1957.

Alexander Rogers and Henry Beveridge (Trs.) *Tuzuk-e-Jehangiri* Munshi Ram Manohar Lal, Delhi. 1968 (Reprint).

Amarjot Sekhon *Panjabi Novel Da Itihas* Lahore Book Shop, Ludhiana. 1st Edition : Novsmber, 1972.

A.M. Hocart, *Kingship* Watts and Co. London, 1941.

A.S. Altekar *State and Government in Ancient India.* Moti Lal Banarsi Dass, New Delhi. Third Edition : 1958.

A,S. Beveridges (Trs.) *Memoirs of Babur* (Translation of *Tuzuk-e-Babri*) Oriental Books Reprint Corpn. New Delhi. 1979 (First published in London : 1912)

Ashfaq Ahmad Azmi, *Nazir Ahmad* : *Shakhsiyat Aur Karname*, Muktaba Shahraha. Urdu Bazar, Delhi. First Edition : 1974.

Aurbindo *Sri Aurbindo Birth Centenary Volumes.* Sri Aurbindo Ashram, Pandicherry 1975.

Aurbindo Ghosh and Barindar Kumar Ghosh (Trs.) *Anandmaṭh*, Basumanti Sahitya Mandir Calcutta, 1910.

Ādi Granth, Sri Damdami Bīṛ various printed editions standard pagination 1430 pp.

Balbir Singh, *Kalam Di Karamat*, Khalsa Samacar, Amritsar. July 1975 –

—*Lammi Nadar* Khalsa Samacar, Amritsar 2nd Edition

1975 (Ist Edition : 1953)

Bertrand Russell *Power* Unwin Russell, Books, London. 1963.

Bhagat Singh *Sikh Polity in the Eighteenth and Nineteenth Centuries* Oriental Publishers and Distributors, New Delhi. 1978.

Bipin Chandra, *Modern India* NCERT New Delhi. Reprinted December, 1986. (First published in 1971).

Brijendra Nath Bandyopadhyay and Sajnikacita (Edts) *Alaler Gharer Dulal* Bangiya Sahitya Priśad. Calcutta. 1940-1947.

Chandu Manon, *Indulekha* Caxton Press, Kohikkotu 1889.

Dasam Granth Sikh Reference Library, Amritsar.

Davinder Singh Duggal, (Eng. Trs.) *Bijai Singh* Hemkunt Press, New Delhi. First published : October 1983.

Edward. J. Thompson, *Rabindra Nath Tagore His Life anh Work* Y.M.C.A. Pubishing House, Calcutta, 1921.

E. Denison Rose, (Ed) *Fakhar-ud-Din's Tarikh-e-Mubarak Shahi*, London 1927.

Edward Thomas, *The Chronicles of the Pathan Kings of Delhi* Munshi Ram Manohar Lal, New Delhi 1967.

Edwin R.A. Seligman (Ed) *Enclopaedia of Social Sciences* The Macmillan and Co, Canada April, 1935 (First published in 1931)

Elias and Ross (Trs.) *Tarikh-e-Rashid* Academic Asiatica, Delhi 1973.

Ernest Trumpp. (Trs.) *The Adi Granth* Munshi Ram Manohar Lal, Delhi. Edition : August, 1970 (First published in 1877).

Gaganinder Kaur, *Bhai Vir Singh De Navelan Te Singh Sabha Lehar Da Prabhav* Lahore Book Shop, Ludhiana March 1984.

Ganda Singh *History of the Gurdwata of Shahid Ganj, Lahore*, Pub. Author, December, 1935.

……(Ed.) *Panjab* Panjabi Sahit Academy, Ludhiana, 1962.

……(Ed) *The Panjab Past and Present* Oct. 1970 Vol. IV Part II, Patiala,

…(Ed) *Bhai Vir Singh* (Birth Centenary Volume), Publication Bureau, Panjabi University, Patiala. (Panjab Past and Present Vol. VI, Part 2, October 1972 Sr. No. 12) 1984, (Reprint)

……(Ed.) *Early European Accounts of the Sikhs* Indian Studies Past and Present, Calcutta March 1982.

……(Ed) *The Singh Sabha and Other Socio-Religious Movements in the Panjab*, Panjabi University Publication Bureau, Patiala, Second Edition : 1984.

George Forester, *A Journey From Bengal to England*, R. Faulder, New Bond Street, London, 1798. 2 Vols.

George Rawlinson, *Five Great Monarchies of the Ancient Eastern World* 4 Vols. J. Murray, London. 1862-1867.

G.E. Ward (Trs.) *The Bride's Mirror* Henry Frowde, Loudon, 1903.

Giani Mahan Singh, *Khalsa Samacar* Vol. 51; No. 43; 1950.

Gobind Singh Mansukhani (Eng. Trs) *Sundri* Hemkunt Press, New Delhi. May, 1983.

Gokul Chand Narang *Transformation of Sikkim* New

Book Society of India, New Delhi Fifth Edition, 1960 (First published in 1912)

Gopal Singh, *Panjabi Sahit Da Itihas*, Eastern Panjab Publishers New Delhi, Second Edition : 1950.

......*A History of the Sikh People* World Book Centre, New Delhi. 2nd Revised Edition : 1988 (First Edition : 1979)

Gopi Nath T.A. Rao *Elements of Hindu Ieonography* Indological Book House, Delhi. Second Fdition 1971 (First Edltion : New York, (1914).

G.S. Dhillon *Character and Impact of the Singh Sabha Movement in the Hlstory of the Panjab.* Panjabi University Library, Patiala (Ph D. Thesis).

G.S. Khosla, *Bhai Vir Singh* Heritage Publisher's India, New Delhi. 1984.

Gurbachan Singh Talib, *Guru Nanak : His Personality and Vision.* Gurdas Kapur and Sons, Delhi, 1969.

......Gurbachan Singh Talib (Ed.) *Bhai Vir Singh : Life Times and Works.* Publication Bureau, Panjab University, Chandigarh Firsl Edition : 1973.

Harbans Singh *Bhai Vir Singh* Sahitya Akademi New Delhi, 1972.

Harbhajan Singh *Gurmukhi Lipi Mein Hindi Kavya* Bharti Sahit Mandir, Delhi 1963.

Hari Ram Gupta, *History of the Sikhs* (vol. II) Munshi Ram Manohar Lal, Delhi. Third Revised Edition ; 1978 (First publised in 1937).

……*History of Sikh Gurus* Uttar Chand Kapur and Sons, New Delhi 1973.

Humayun Kabir *Indian Heritage* Asia Publishing House, Bombay 1964.

Ibn Hassan *The Central Structure of Mughal Empire* Oxford University Press 1936,

Inder Singh Gill (Ed.) *Sri Gur Bilas Patshaib*, Wazir Hind Press, Amritsar, 1968.

Indu Bhushan Bannerjee, *The Evolution of Khalsa* A Mukerjee and Co. (P) Ltd. Calcutta. Vol. I Edition : Second, May, 1963.

Jagjit Singh, The *Sikh Revolution* Bahri Publications (P) Ltd., New Delhi 1981.

James Starchey (Gen. Ed.) *The Complete Psychological Works of Sigmund Freud.* The Hogrth Press Ltd., London 1965. (First published in 1953) Vol. VII.

Jaswant Singh Neki, *Ardas*, *Roop Darśan*, *Abhias* Singh Brothers, Mai Sewan, Amritsar, 1989.

Jawahar Lal Nehru *The Discovery of India* Meridian Book Ltd., London 1960.

Jayanti Chattopadhyah, "The Villain in the Nineteenth Century Bengali Literature," paper presented in the Weekly Seminar of the Department of Modern Indian Languages, University of Delhi, Delhi on 26.11.1987 (Cyclostyled pp. 9).

Jeet Singh Sital (Ed.) *Sri Guru Panth Prākas* (*of Ratan Singh Bhangu*) Shiromani Gurdwara Ptabandhak Committee, Amritsar, 1984.

J. Estlin Carpenter, *Theism in Medieval India* Oriental Book Corpn., New Delhi 1977 (Reprint) (First published in London: 1921).

J. L. Shastri (Ed.) *Ancient Indian Tradition and Mythology* (*Śiva Purāṇa*). Part II. Moti Lal Banarsi Das, Delhi. Reprint : 1978 (First Edition 1969).

J. Neville Figgis, *The Theory of Divine Right of King*, The University Press, Cambridge, 1896.

Joginder Singh, "Bhai Kahan Singh Hum Hindu Nahin : Polemic or Social Document" in *Journal of Sikh Studies* Vol. XIV No. 1 February 1987. Guru Nanak Dev University, Amritsar.

John Clark Archer, *The Sikhs in Relation of Hindus Christians and Ahmadiyas*, Princeton University Press, Princeton 1946.

John, J. H. Gordon, *The Sikhs*, Blackwood and Sons, London, 1904.

John Martin Honighberger, *Thirty Years in the East* R. C. Lepage & Co. Calcutta, 1852.

Joseph Davey Cunninghnm: *History of the Sikhs* (Edited by H. L. O. Garrett) S. Chand and Co. Delhi, 1966. (Reprint).

J. S. Guleria (Ed.) *Bhai Vir Singh*, Bhai Vir Singh Sahitya Sadan Publication, New Delhi. Second Revised and Enlarged Edition 1984 (First Edition : 1973)

J. Waskom Pickett, *Christian Mass Movement in India* Abingdon Press, New York, 1933.

Kahan Singh Nabha, *Hum Hindu Nahin* Singh Sabha Śtabadi Committee. Amritsar, December. 1973 (Reprint).

Karl Marx and Fredrick Engles "A Contribution to the Critique of Political Economy" in *Seiected Works* Foreign Publishing House, Moscow. Vol. I 1958.

Kern Fritz. *Kingship and Law in the Middle Ages* (translated with Introduction by S. B. Chrimes) Basil Blackwell, Oxford, 1939,

Khaliq Ahmed Nizami and Abdur Rashid (Edts) *Elliot and Dowson's History of India* Cosmopoliton Aligarh First Edition : 1952.

Khalsa Samacar, Amritsar, (varions issues)

Khazan Singh *History of the Sikh Religion*, Language Department Panjab, Patiala, 1970 (First published in 1914).

Khushwant Singh, *A History of the Sikhs* (2 Vol.) Oxford University Press, Delhi 1977 (First published in 1963).

Khushwaqat Rai, *Tawarikh-e-Sikkhan* (or *Kitab-e-Twarikh-Panjab*)

Kirpal Singh *Janam Sakhi Prampra* Panjabi University, Patiala, First Edition : December, 1969.

Kirpal Singh Kasel and other *Panjabi Sahit Di Utpati Te Vikas*,Lahore Book Shop, Ludhiana, 4th Ediition : 1976

Kishan Singh, *Gurbanī Da Sacca*, Sedh Prakashan Delhi First Edition : April 1976.

K. M. Ashraf, *Life and Condition of the People of Hindustan* Munshi Ram Manohar Lal New Delhi Second Edition : 1970.

Krishan Lal (Ed.) *Sri Niwas Dass Granthāvali* Nagri Pracharṇi Sabha, Kashi, Samvat. 2021 (1953 A. C.)

Life of Ramakrishna Advaita Ashram Mayavati, Almora Sixth Edition, 1948.

Lepel Griffin *The Punjab Chief* Civil and Military Government Press. Lahore, 1893. 2 vols.

................*Rajas of the Panjab* Panjab Printing Co. Lahore,

Makatib-e-Iqbal (Letters addressed to Khan Niaz Aldin Khan) Iqbal Akadmi, Lahore (Pakistan), 1986.

Manual of Fundamentals of Marxism—Leninism. Progress Publishers, Moscow 1963.

Maulana Muhammad Najmul Ghani *Tarikh-e-Awadh* Mataba-e-Matla-ul-Uloom, Moradabad, Februray, 1909.

Max Arthur Macauliffe *The Sikh Religion* (6 Vols) S. Chand and Co. Delhi. First Indian Edition : 1963. (First published in 1909).

Max Weber, *The Sociology of Religion* (translated by Epharaim Fischoff) Methuen and Co. Ltd. London, 1965 First German Edition. 1922).

Muhammad Habid, *Sultan Mahmud of Ghaznin* S. Chand add Co. Delhi Second Edition : 1951.

Narendra Nath Law (Ed.) *Indian Historical Quarterly* Calcutta Oriental Press, Calcuttar Vol, XIII 1937.

N. Gerald Barrier, *The Sikhs and their Literature* Manohar Book Service Delhi, 1970.

Nur Ahmad Chishti, *Tahqiqat-e-Chisti*, Lahore, 1906.

Prakash Singh, *Gantinuning infinence of Bhai Vir Singh*, Singh Brothers, Amritsar, 1972.

Prem Lata, *Swami Dayanand Saraswati* Sumit Publications, New Delhi, 1990.

P. Sethu Madhav Rao, (Abridged and Trs.) *Tahmas Nama*, Bombay, 1967.

R. P. Tripathi, *Some Aspects of Muslim Administration* Central Book Depot, Allahabab 1964.

S. A. A. Rizvi, *The Wonder that was India* (Vol.2) Sidgwick and Jackson, London, 1987.

Santokh Singh, 'Importance of Amrit' in *Sikh Review* 23(258), June 1975.

Sant Singh Sekhon *Bhai Vir Singh Te Una Da Yug* Lahore Book Shop Ludhiana September 1962.

Satbir Singh, *Puratan Itihasak Jiwnian*, New Book Co. Jullundur, 1969.

Satinder Singh, *Bhai Vir Singh Jiwan Te Racna* Publication Bureau, Panjabi University, Patiala 1982.

Sayyid Safdar Hussain *Lucknow Ki Tehzibi Miras* Bargahe Adab, Haider Road, Lahore, 1975.

Shamsher Singh Ashok, *Panjab Dian Lehran* Kaviraj Narain Singh Vallabh Himat Puri, 1954.

Sharif Ahmed, *Abdul Halim Sharar : Life and His Works* (in Urdu) Ph.D. Thesis. Unyublished Type MS. Delhi University Library, New Delhi. Accession No. Th. 3131.

Sher Singh, *Philosophy of Sikhism*, Sikh University Press Lahore, 1944.

Sisir Kumar Das *The Artist In Chains : The Life of Bankim Chandra Chatterjee* New Statesman Publishing Co. New Delhi. First Edition : 1984.

S. M. Latif, *History of Panjab* Central Press Ltd., Calcutta 1891.

Sohan, *Gur Bilas Patshahi* 6, Bhasha Vibhag, Panjab, Patiala, 1972.

Stephen D. Dunning. 'The Sikh Religion : An Examination of Some of the Western Studies" in *Journal of Religious Studies* Panjabi University Patiala Vol. II Autumn 1970.

Sunder Lal *San Satawan* Anjnman Tariq-e-Urdu, Hind. Aligarh. Decemberi 1957.

Surinder Singh Dusanjh, *Panjabi Itihasik Novel* Sirjina Press Ludhiana. First Edition December, 1969.

Surinder Singh Johar, *The Heritage of Amritsar* Sandeep Prakashan, New Delhi, 1978.

Surinder Singh Kohli, *Panjabi Sahit Da Itihas*. Lahore Book Shop Ludhina, 4th Edition : March, 1955

……A Critical Study of Adi Granth The Panjabi Writers Cooperative Industrial Society, Ltd., New Delhi, March, 1961.

……(Ed.) *Bhai Vir Singh Commemomorative Issue of Parkh* Panjab University, Chahdigarh, 1972.

……(Ed.) *Bhai Vir Singh Jiwan Sama Te Racna*, Publication Bureau, Panjab University, Chandigarh First Edition : 1973.

Swami Dayanand, *Satyarth Prākāś* Vedic Mantralya, Ajmer, 1990 (Samvat.)

Swinder Singh Uppal, *Panjabi Navel : Vidhi Te Vicar* Panjabi Writers Co-operative. New Delhi, 1982.

Tara Chand *Influence of Islam on Indian Culture*. The Indian Press (Publicatians) (P) Ltd., Allahabad, 1993.

Teja Singh and Ganda Singh, *A Short History of the Sikhs* Orient Langmana. India 1950.

Thomas Patrick (Ed.) *Dictionary of Islam* Rupa and Co. Delhi 1988 (First published in 1885).

Trilochan Singh et el (Trs.) *Selectians From the Sacred Writings of the Sikhs* George Allen and Unwin Ltd. London 1960.

Trilochan Singh, *Guru Tegh Bahadur* Gurdwara Prabandha Committee. Chandni Chowk, Delhi, 1967.

T. W. Clark (Ed.) *The Novel in India* George Allen and Unwin Ltd., London 1970.

Vishwa Nath Tiwari, *Vir Singh Sandnarbh Kośa* Publication Bureau, Panjab Univhrsity, Chandigarh.

W. Dumergul (Trs.) *Indulekha* Addison and Co. Madras, 1890, Reprinted by Matur Bhumi, Calcutta, 1965.

W. H. Mcleod, *Guru Nanak and the Sikh Religion* Oxford University Press, 1968.

W. L. M'Greger, *The History of the Sikhs* James Madden, London, 1846, 2 vols.

Yusuf Hussain, *Glimpses of Medieval Indian Culture*, Asia Publishing House, Bombay, Second Edition : 1959.

———

NAME INDEX

— — —

GENERAL INDEX

ERRATA

Page	Line	Incorrect	Correct
6	1	emotienal	emotional
,,	31	oppointment	appointment
12	5	querry	query
16	6	deliberateyl	deliberately
19	18	ith	with
20	14	polıtices	politics
2ʾ	18	unapproingly	unapprovingly
31	28	stemed	stemmed
32	14	accordiag	according
36	30	diciplined	disciplined
51	2	Multun	Multan
59	3	conatitute	constitute
60	6	Decenber	December
,,	29	at least	at last
61	5	against	on
62	19	wamen	women
63	10	Sanib	Sahib
,,	16	injuties	injuries
,,	21	revengc	revenge
64	23	hot	not
78	17	ꝑersuation	persuasion
79	32	paralize	paralyze
82	12	thr	the
88	7	againsl	against
89	31	cacompanied	accompanied
90	7	ambivlence	ambivelence
,,	8	flirstly	firstly

91	20	remainds	reminds
93	27	accouut	account
99	22	Rcalising	Realising
101	28	Charistian	Christian
107	19	eoaxing	coaxing
,,	27	insteal	instead
108	23	denigrte	denigrate
109	1	assissination	assassination
,,	19	visulize	visualise
110	14	blanckned	blackened
112	31	uptill	upto
113	17	viccory	viceroy
115	28	she	the
117	16	Brilish	British
124	10	*msls*	*misals*
125	6	sonspicuouslp	conspicously
,,	13	biogragical	biographical
,,	24	tnings	things
126	17	abobt	about
129	15	tanets	tenets
132	18	satisfactority	satisfactorily
,,	24	affices	affices
133	14	cometent	competent
135	8	conveated	converted
,,	24	collaberation	collaboration
137	30	reiteraned	reiterated
138	6	swaml	Swami
,,	19	Rajha	Ranjha